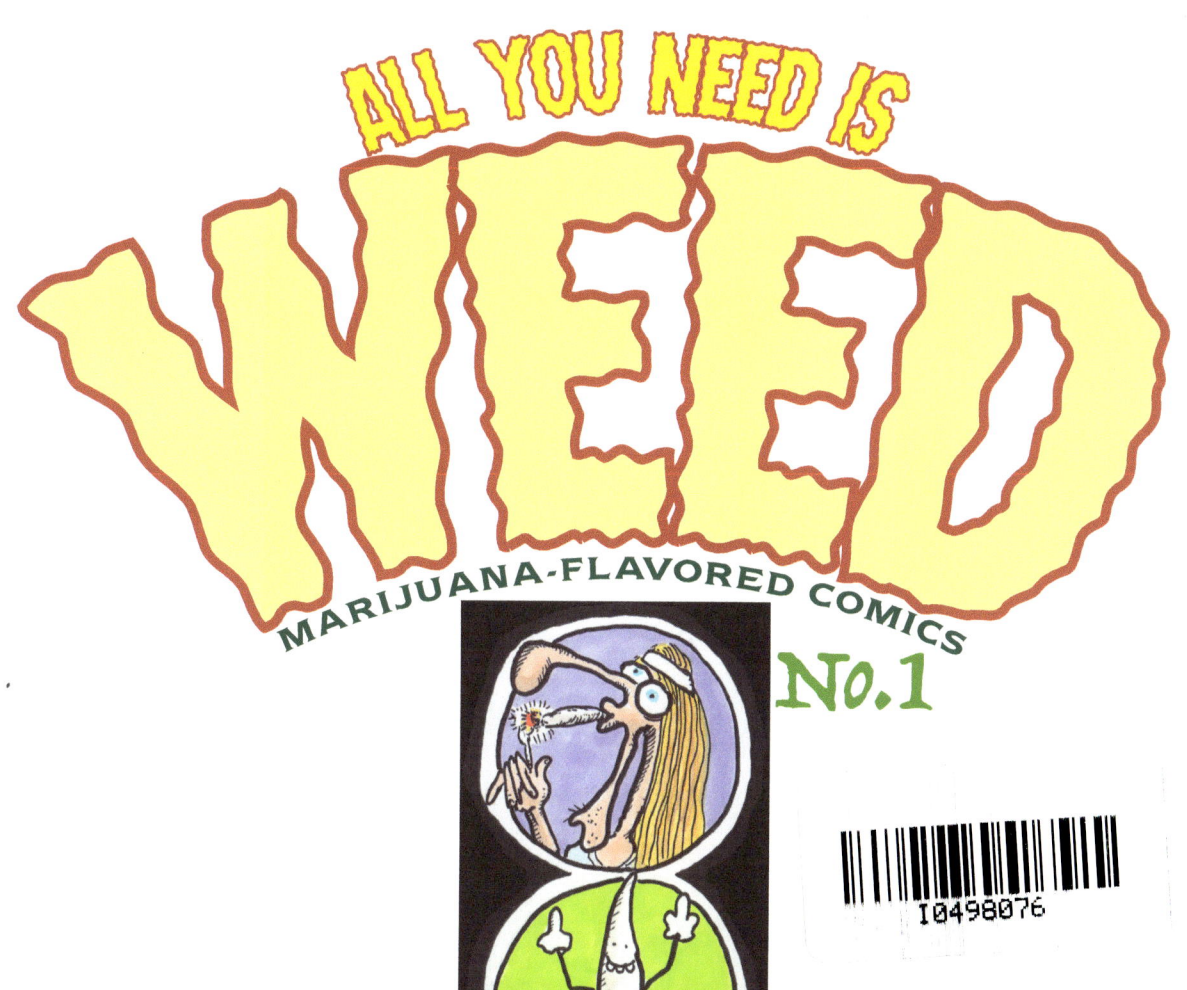

Dedicated to all the true stoners of the world!

* Music listened to while creating these strips: **CSN & Y,** Led Zeppelin, **David Bowie,** T.Rex, **Tom Petty,** Steely Dan, Ramones, **Alice Cooper, Greta Van Fleet,** Queen, **Aerosmith**

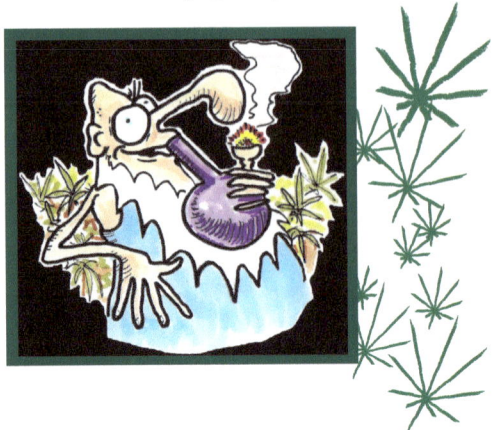

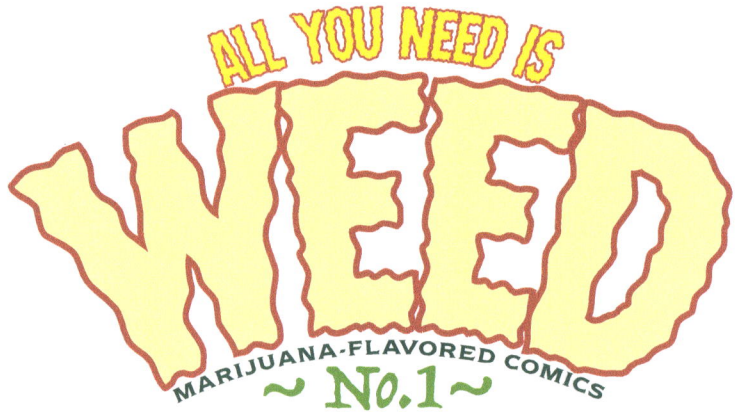

Written, Illustrated, and Designed by Tom Athanasiou

Copyright © 2018 by Thomas Andrew Athanasiou
Tommy Pop Art, LLC
All Rights Reserved.

www.Facebook.com/**AllYouNeedIsWeedComics**
www.**AllYouNeedIsWeedComics**.com
www.**TommyPopArt**.com

CONTENTS

4	FORWARD
6	WHO IS WHO? FEATURING THE A.Y.N.I.W. WORLD
7	MAKE AMERICA GREEN AGAIN! FEATURING GRANDDADDY
11	MUNCHIE COME HOME FEATURING 69
12	SEEDS OF THE GODS FEATURING 69
16	TWILIGHT STONED FEATURING 69
17	WATCH CAT FEATURING CHRONIC GREEN GANG
18	TWILIGHT STONED FEATURING 69
20	COMIC-CON COSMIC BONG FEATURING GRANDDADDY
21	MOTHER LOAD FEATURING CHRONIC GREEN GANG
26	GAME OF BONES FEATURING JONNY THE JOINT
22	BETTER INGREDIENTS FEATURING MELODY WEED
24	COMIC STRIPS 1
23	DOG POT HASH FEATURING MUNCHIE
26	THE GREAT ESCAPE FEATURING JONNY THE JOINT
28	BIG LIPS FEATURING 69
30	THE TRANS "POT" ER FEATURING 69
31	INTERVIEW WITH TOM ATHANASIOU
34	COMIC STRIPS 2
35	ALIENS AMONG GRASS FEATURING GRANDDADDY
36	ABOUT THE ARTIST
39	COMING NEXT...
40	SHIRT SWAG

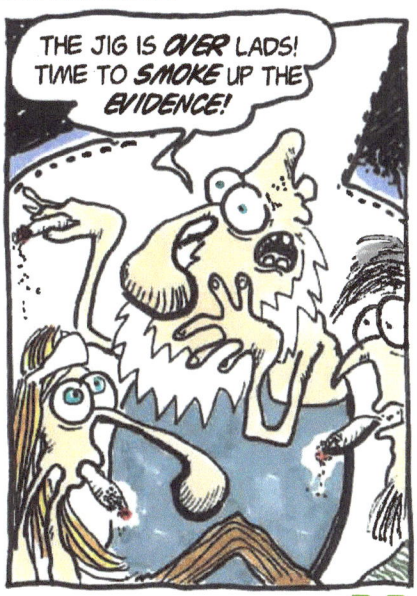

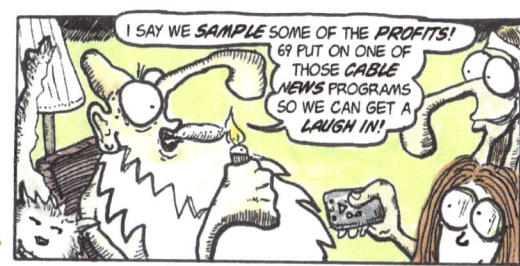

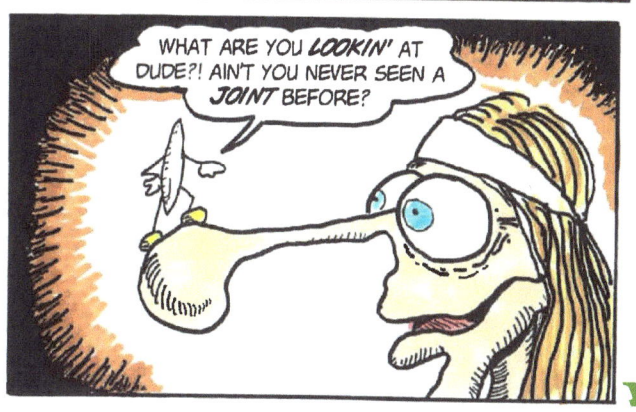

FORWARD

Well, it's been over one year since I published the first introdution issue of ***ALL YOU NEED IS WEED*** which was a hand picked batch of my original black and white strips. We've sold a nice bundle to all our "420" fans online and at all the events and conventions we do through out the year. But if I hear, "Is this a coloring book?" one more time at our non-comic shows, someone is going down!

For this volume I have created some new stories, and have "colorized" most of the marijuana themed stories and strips from the original book. So if you have the first intro issue, I can only hope you will enjoy the hand colored versions. I did all these strips the old fashioned way done in the 70's, all rendered with color ink markers, which in my case, is to maintain *that* classic comic look. People always ask me why I do these and I always tell them the same answer, "I do it because it's fun! I enjoy creating stories and doing what I love to do which is making art, that just happens to be fun cannibis-based comics."

I hope you enjoy my stories and strips that I have created for this — my second, but kinda the first official "pot" concentrated collection, and in full-color! So ignite that bowl (of the good stuff) and start reading!

Tom Athanasiou
June 2018

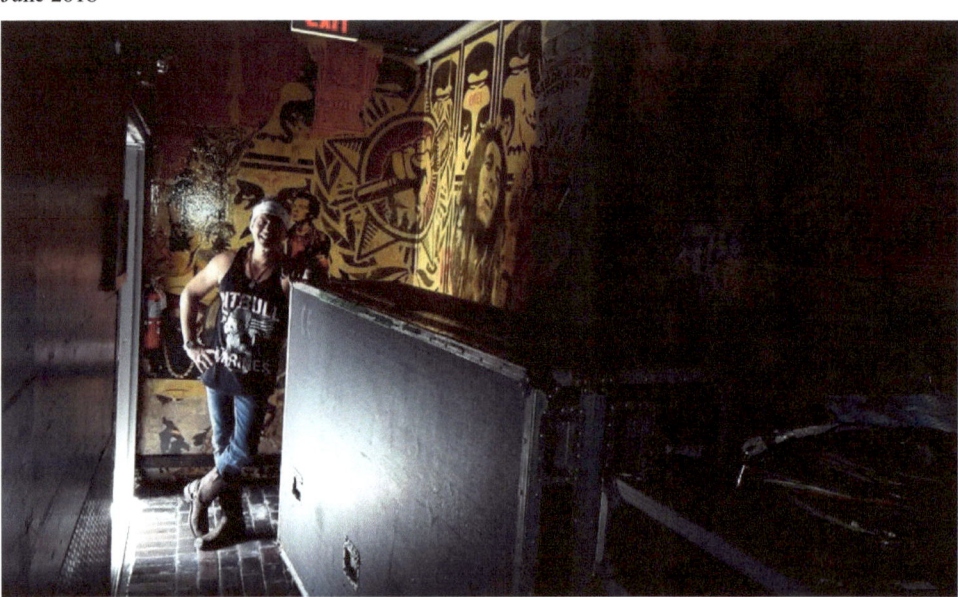

ALL YOU NEED IS WEED

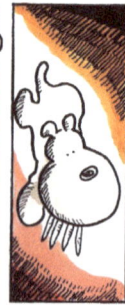
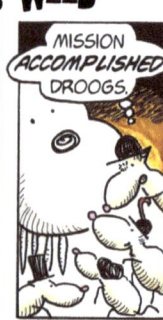
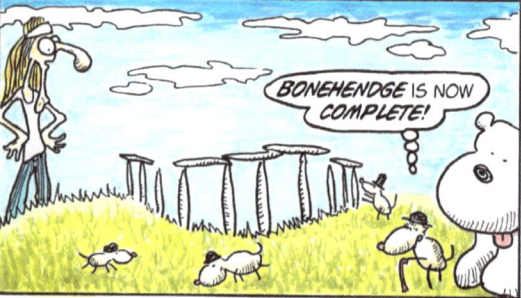

No.1: The first A.Y.N.I.W. strip done in full-color.

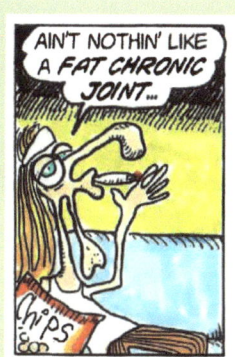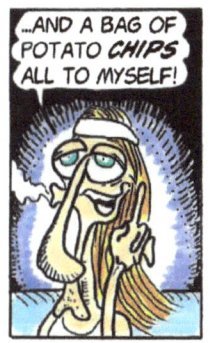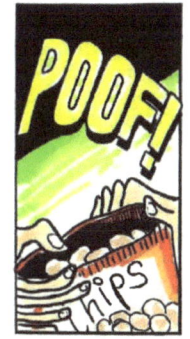

"ALL YOU NEED IS WEED
WEED IS ALL YOU NEED"
TOM ATHANASIOU

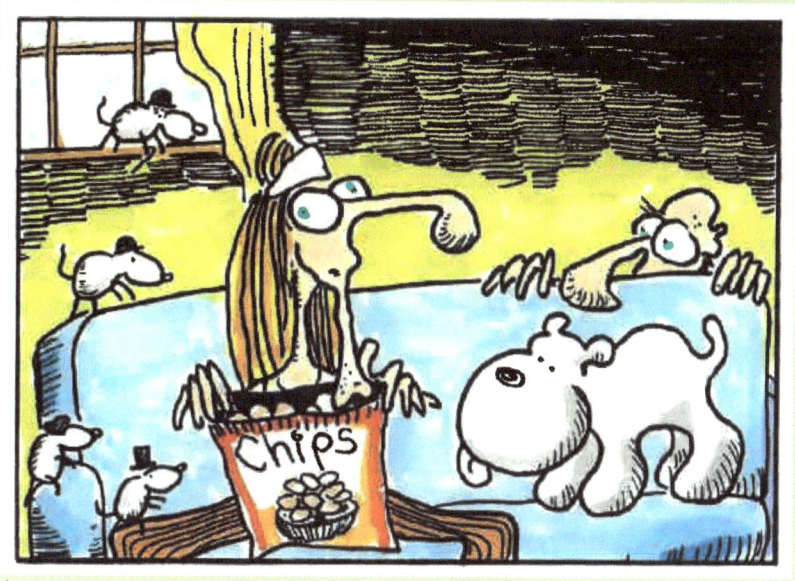

*...AND SOME GOOD FRIENDS!

WHO IS WHO?

We'll keep this short and simple. I mean, come on, it's a pot influenced comic book peeps! 69, Woody, Jonny The Joint, they are some of the chronic creatures that dwell on Granddaddy's massive pot farm in Serenity Hills, somewhere in the West region of America. So here it is, a quick bio of these reefer head characters.....

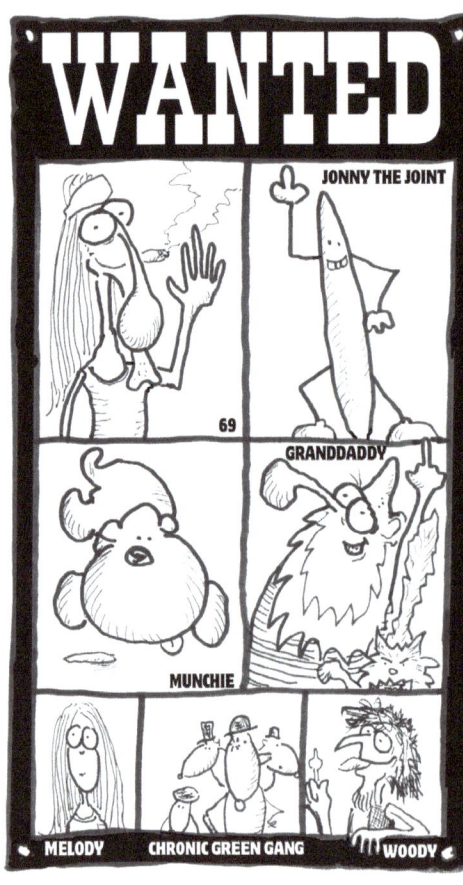

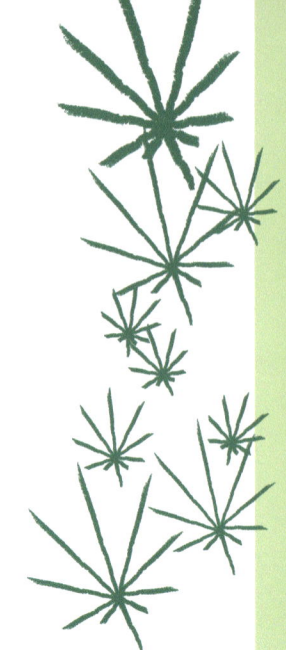

"JUST LOOK AT 'EM! *GUILTY* AS HELL! DAMN *POTHEADS* ARE RUININ' THIS WORLD OF *OURS*. 'SPECIALLY IN THE GOOD OLE *U.S.* OF *'MERICA!*"

FEATURING:
- **69** – THE GUY THAT GROWS THE STUFF
- **WOODY** – HIS STONER BEST FRIEND
- **MUNCHIE** – HIS LOVEABLE ADOPTED PIT BULL
- **MELODY WEED** – 69'S "EDIBLE CANNABIS" BAKER COUSIN
- **GRANDDADDY** – THE OLD FART THAT ACTUALLY OWNS THE FARM
- **CHRONIC GREEN GANG** – BAD MICE DOIN' BAD THINGS
- **JONNY THE JOINT** – ONE NASTY ROLLED WISEASS

Old School Rules: Oh my god. Is that a black and white drawing or a coloring book?!

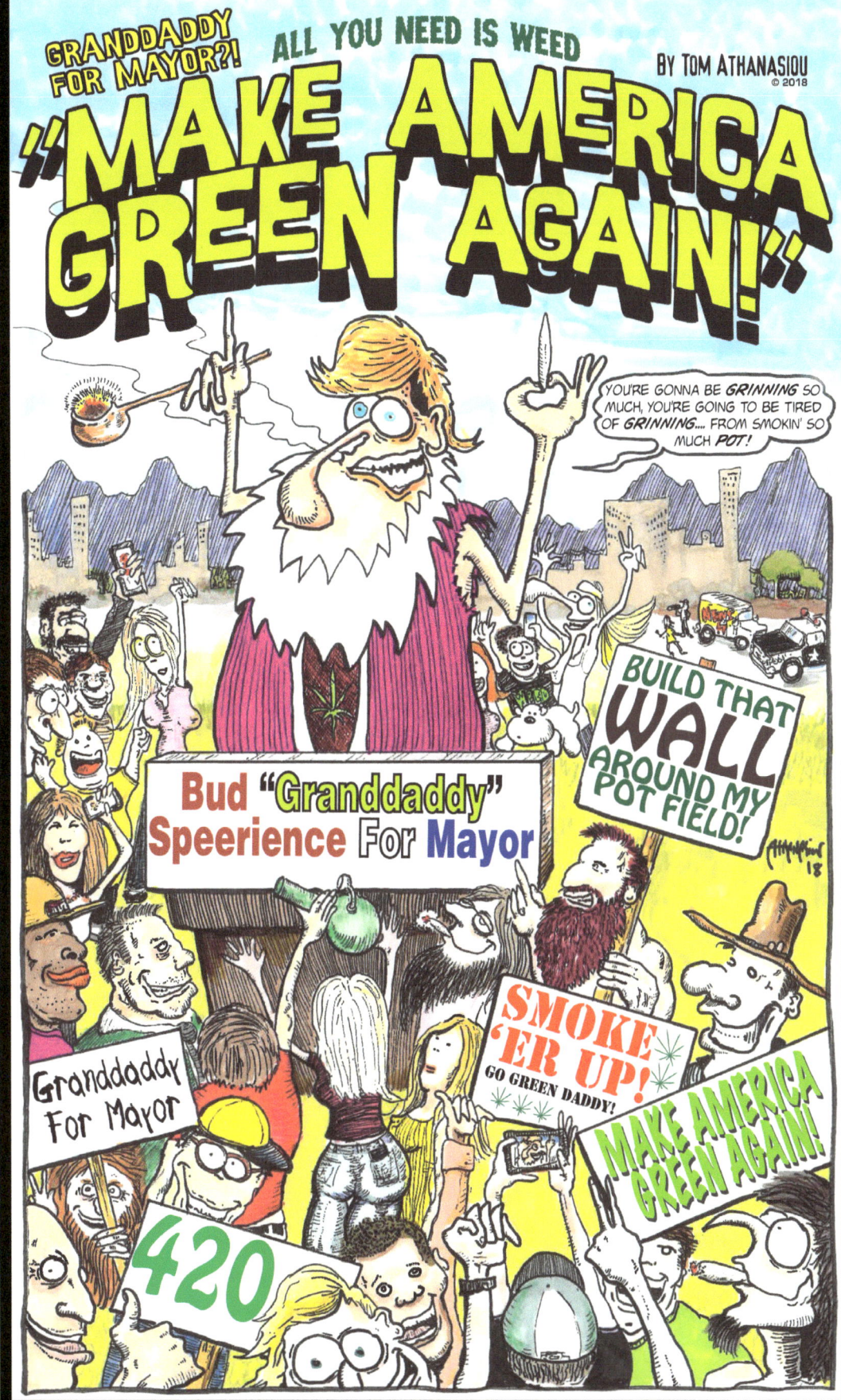

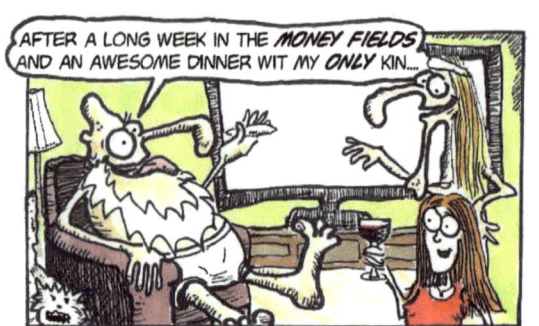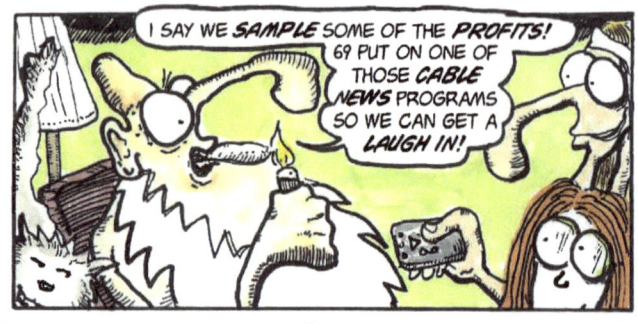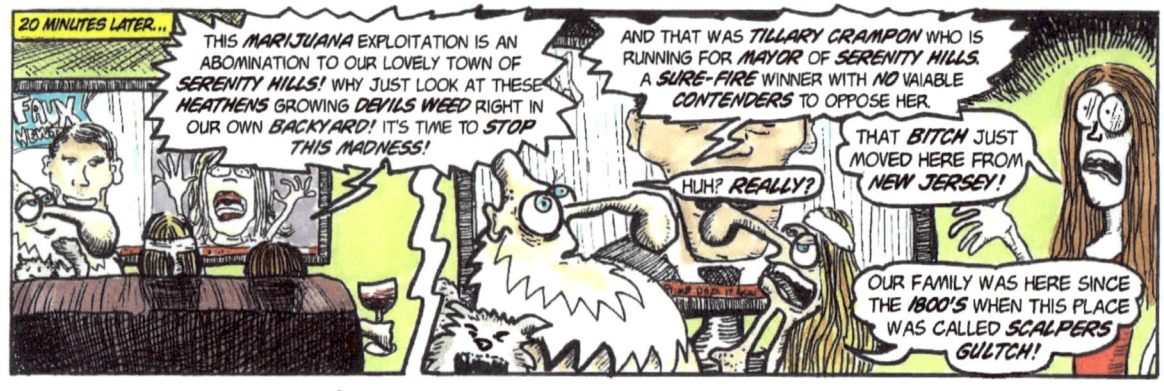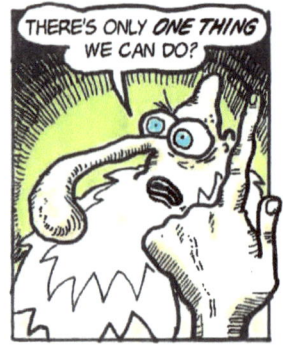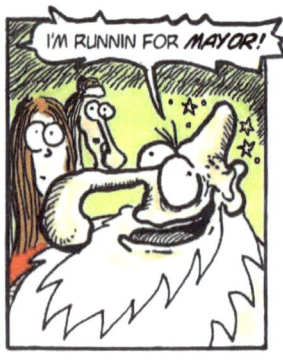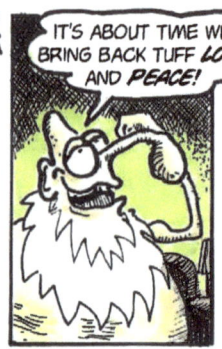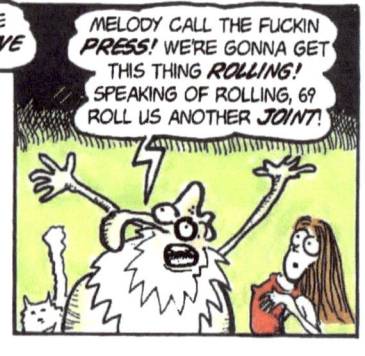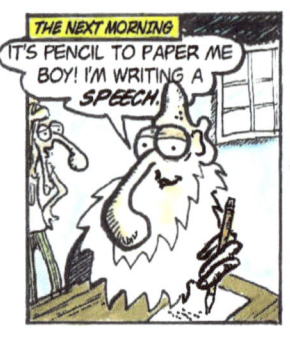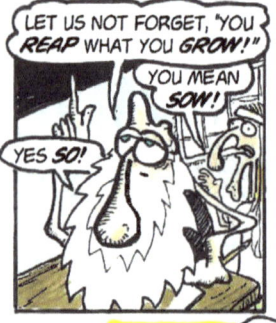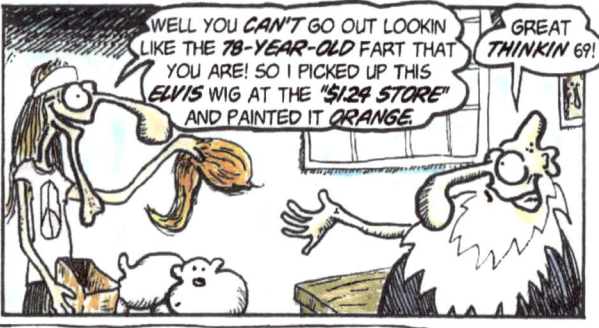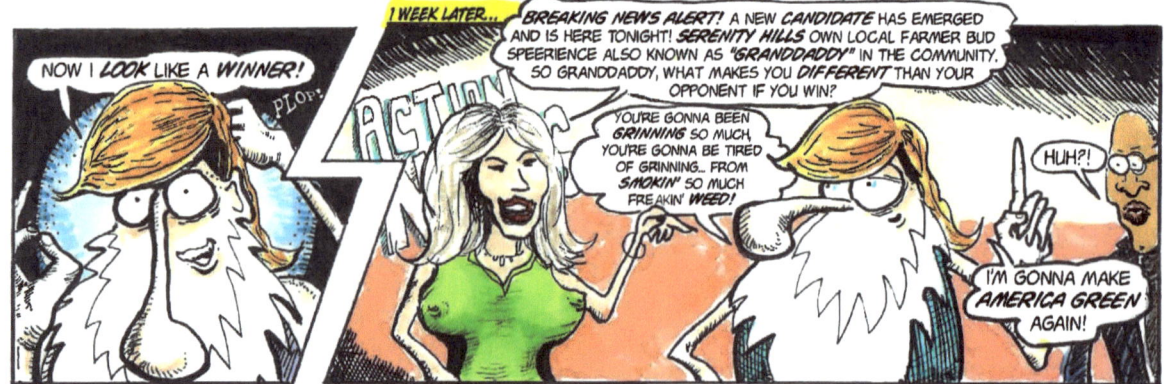

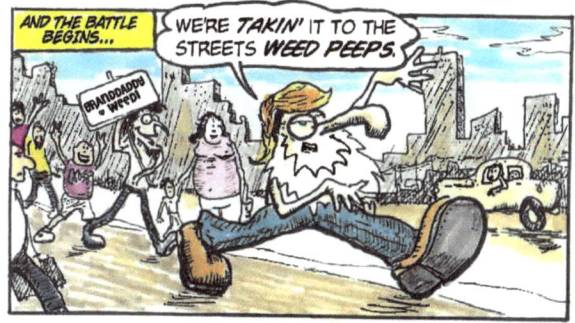
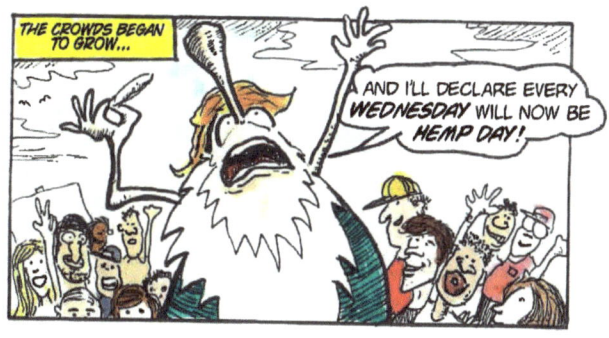
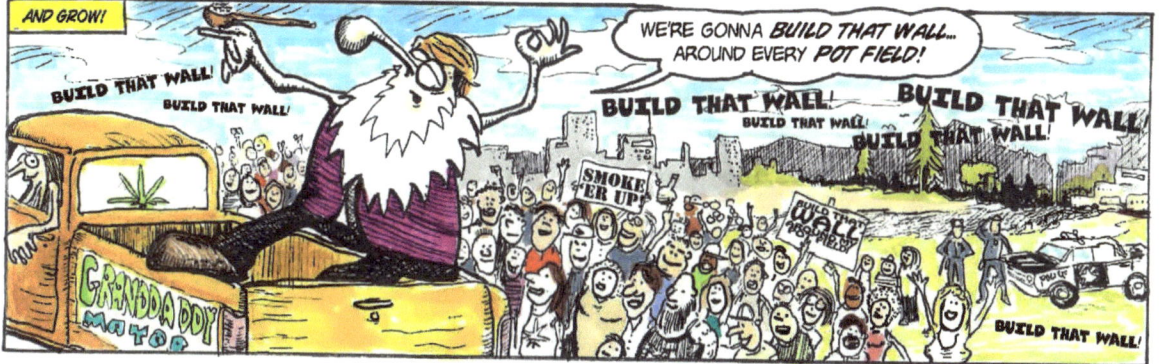
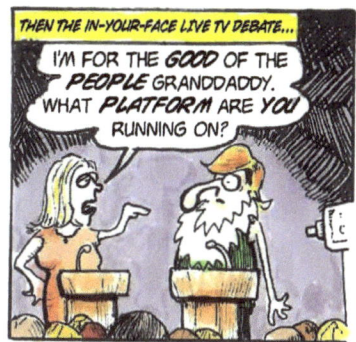
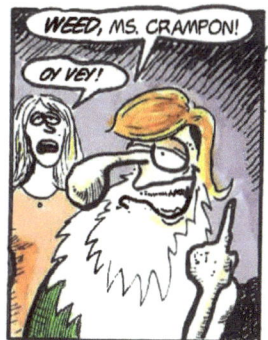
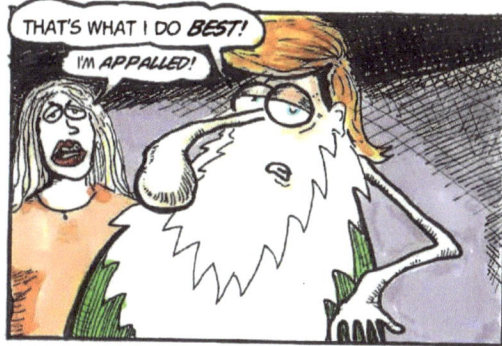
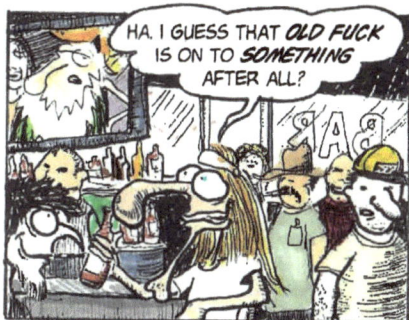
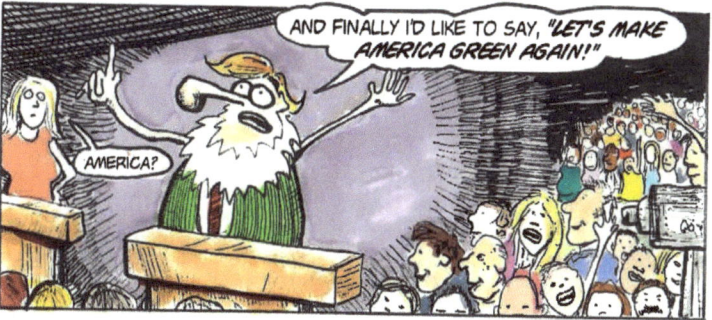
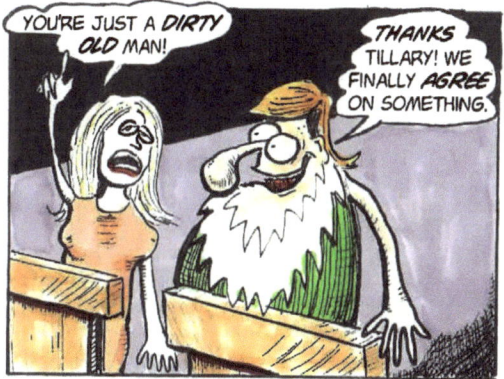
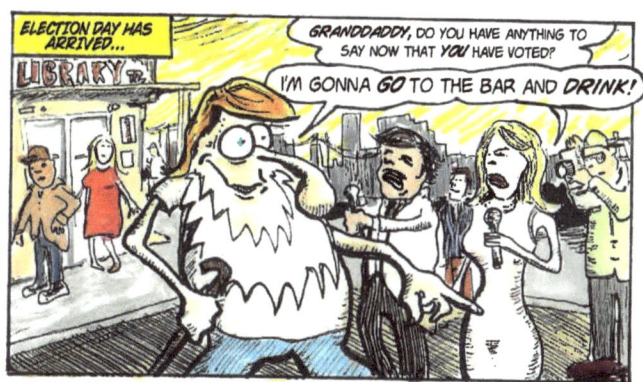

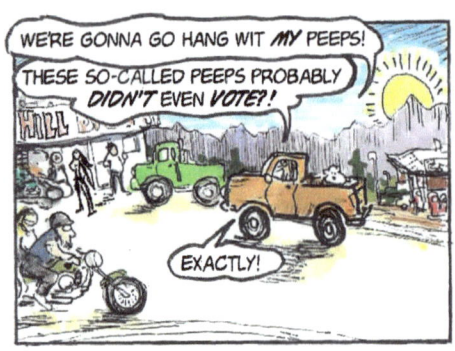
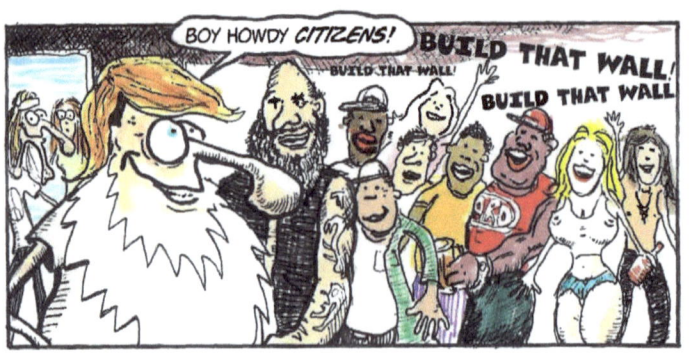
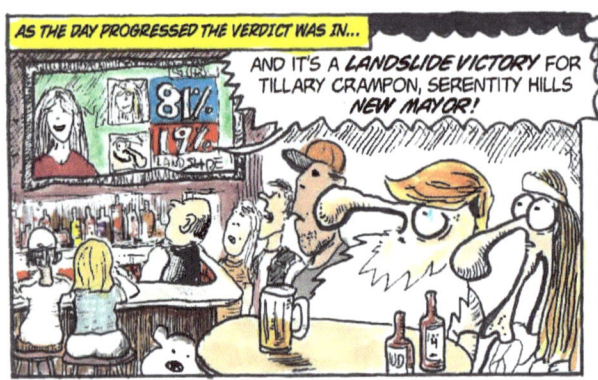
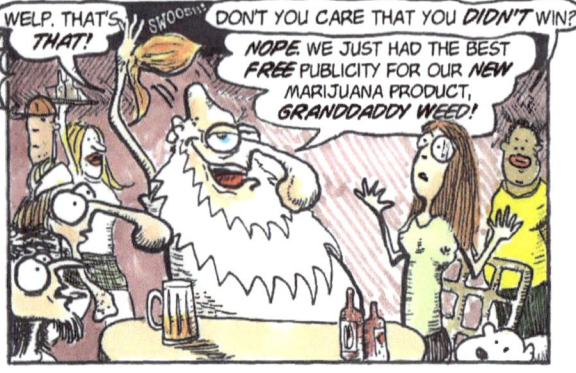
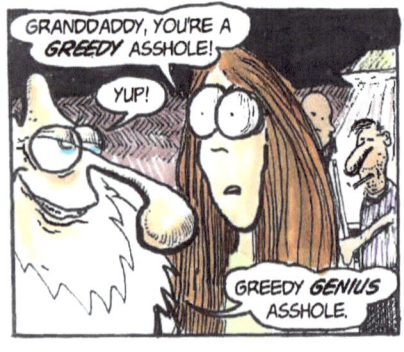
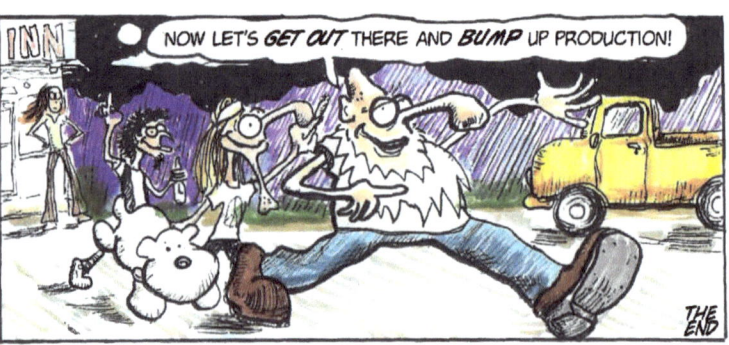
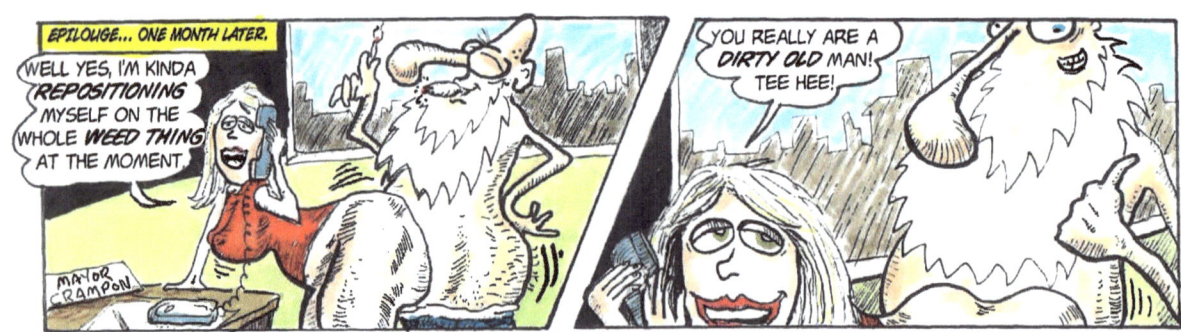
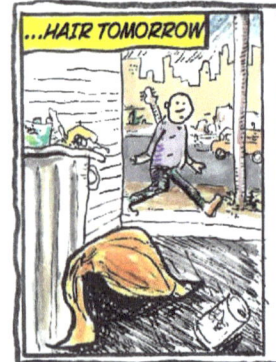
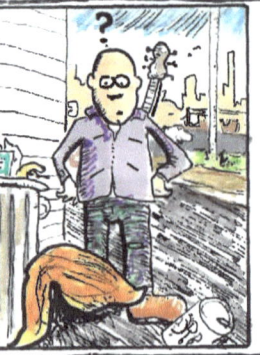
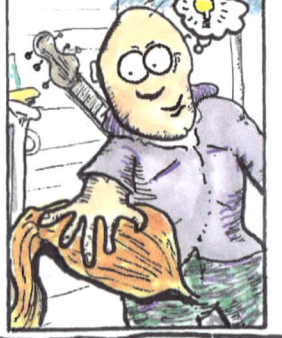
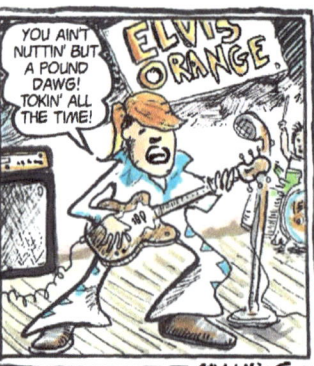

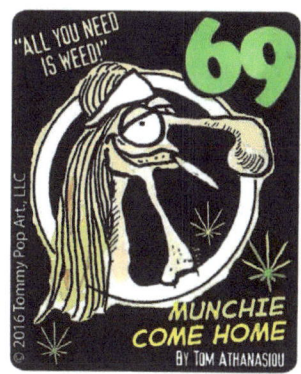
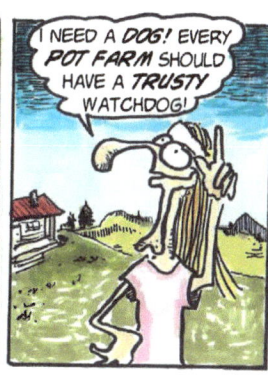
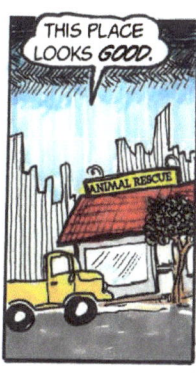
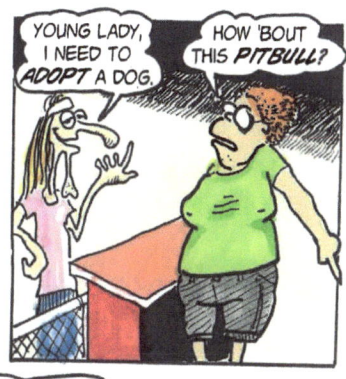
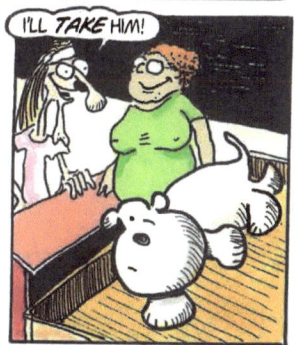
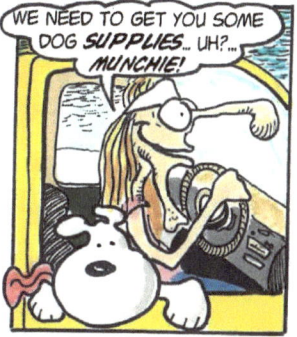
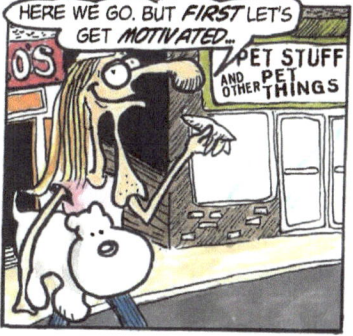
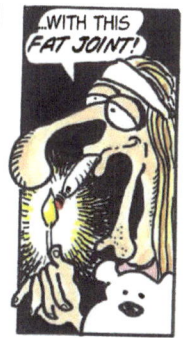
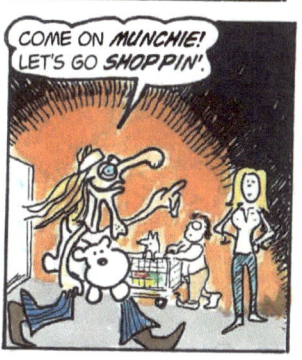
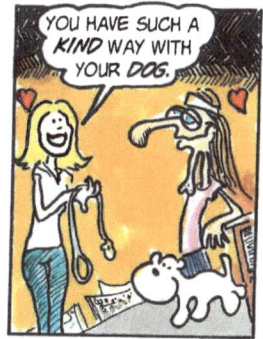
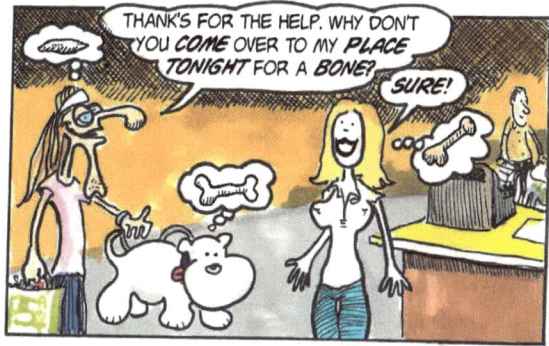
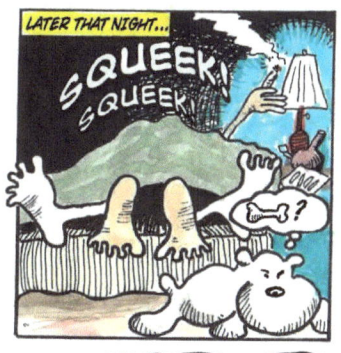
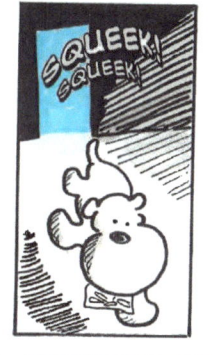
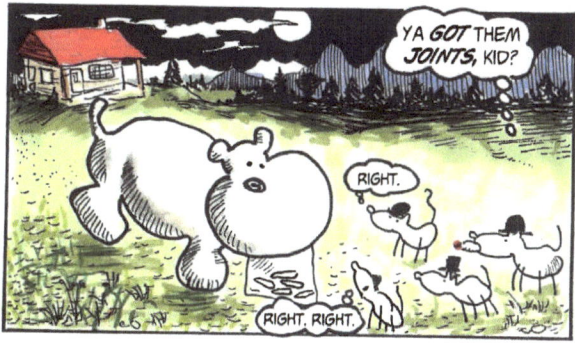
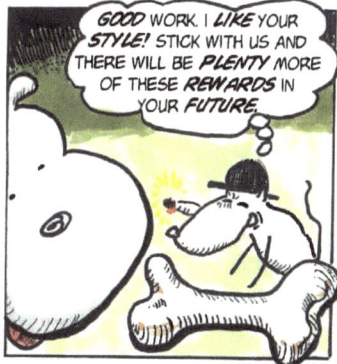
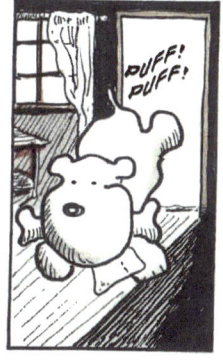
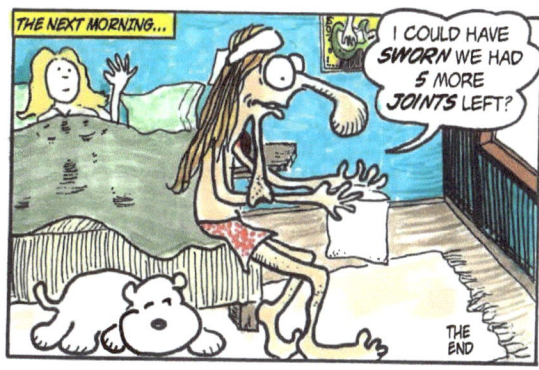

A not so long time ago....

starring in **69**

Seeds of the Gods

BY TOM ATHANASIOU

There is an ancient myth that gods came down from the sky and gave the primitive people a vast treasure trove of knowledge and gold. But there is also the little-known story of the **Seeds Of The Gods**. Once planted, grown, harvested, and smoked, this mysterious, mind-altering herb was described as a dimensional gate-opener spanning far beyond mortal man's comprehension. It was hidden from mankind by the last of the **Mayans**, and thought to be brought into the new continent of America in the vicinity of one so-called pot farm .....

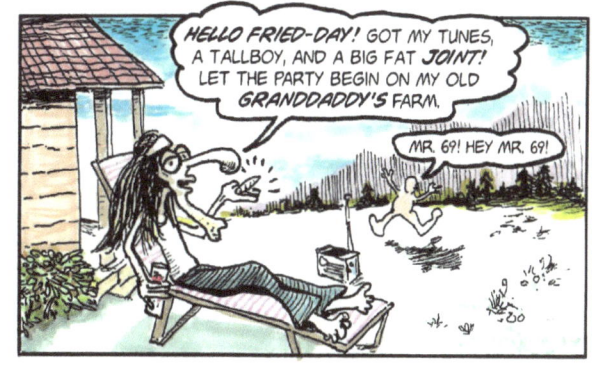
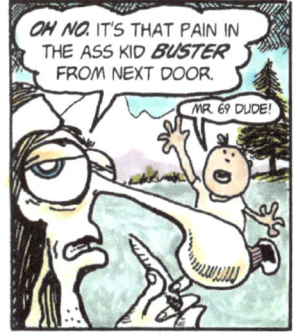
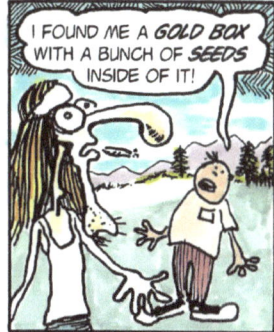
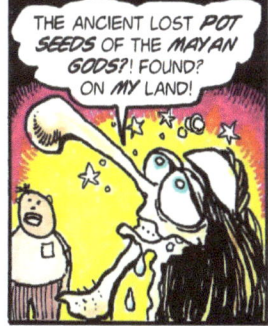
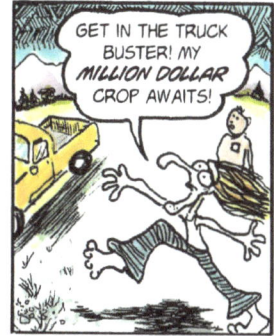
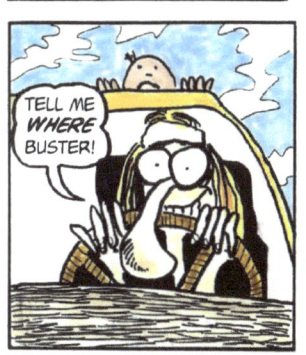
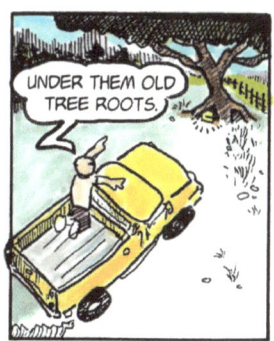
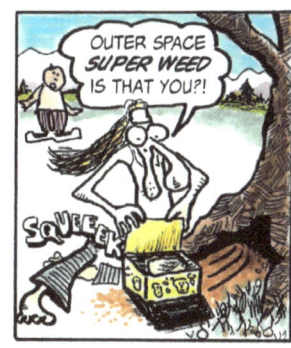
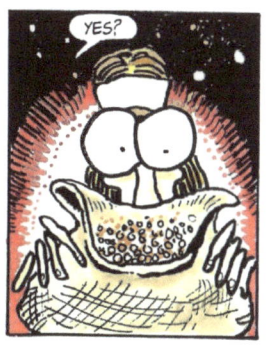
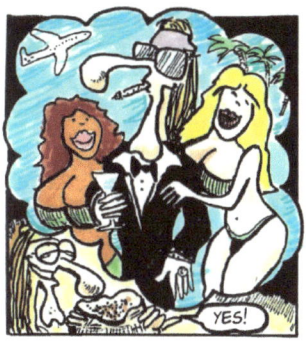
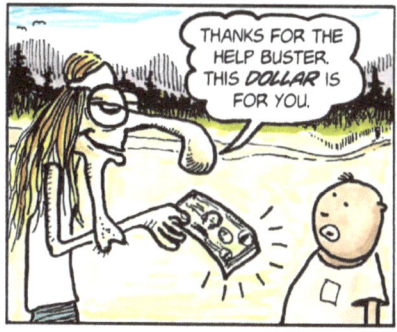
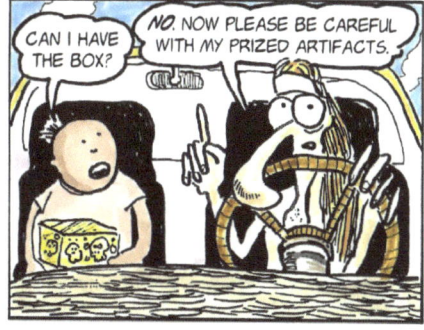
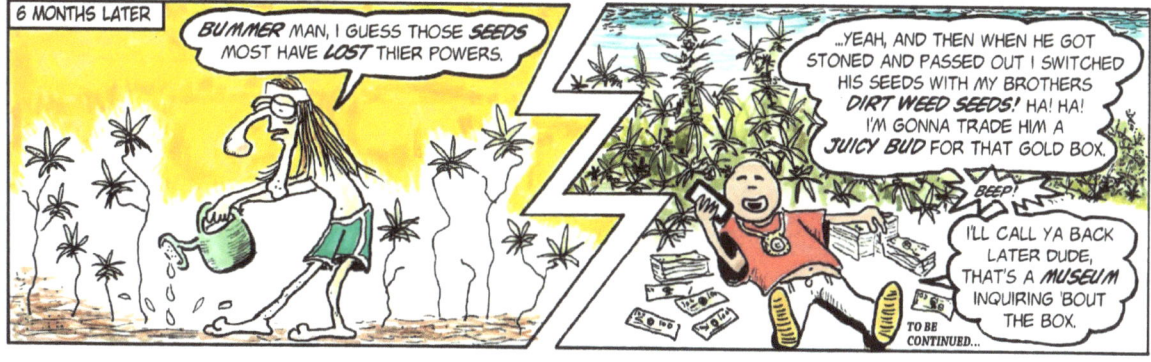

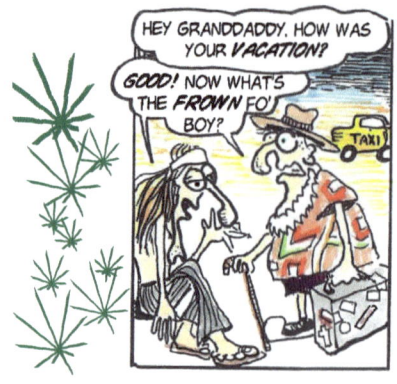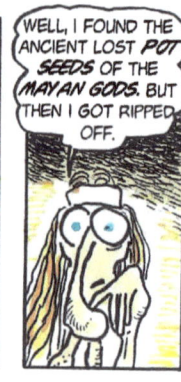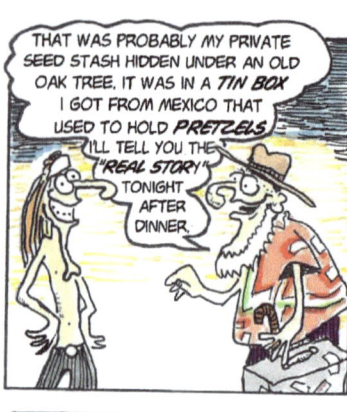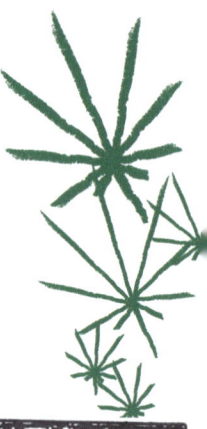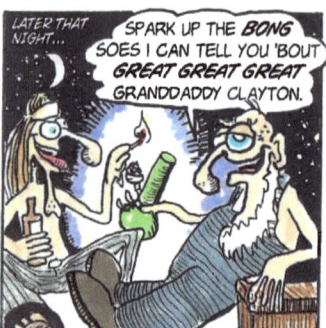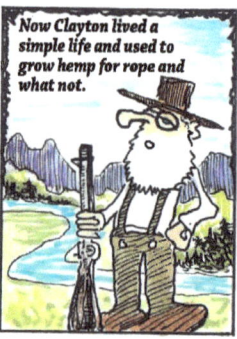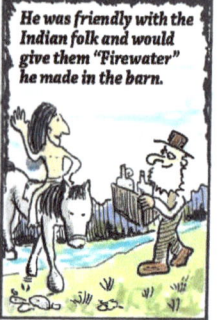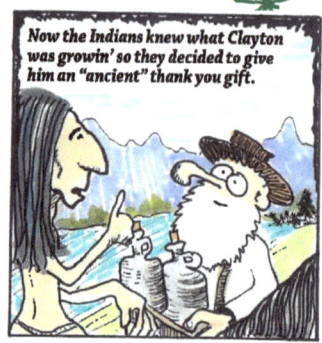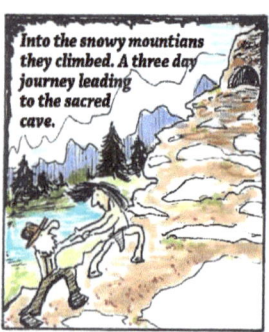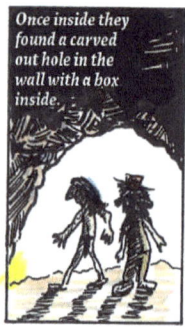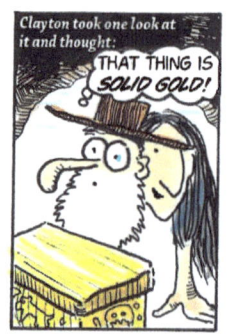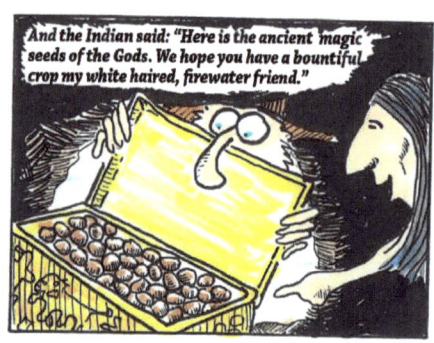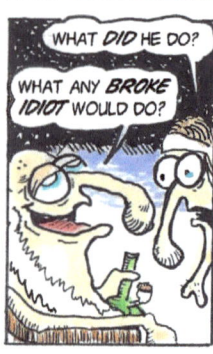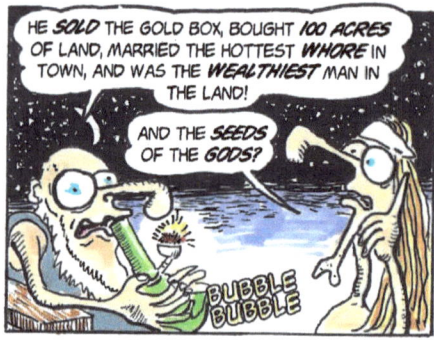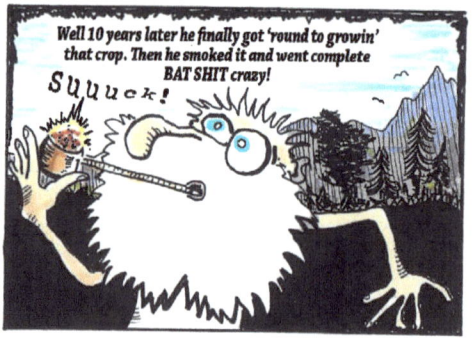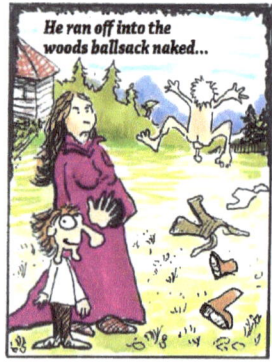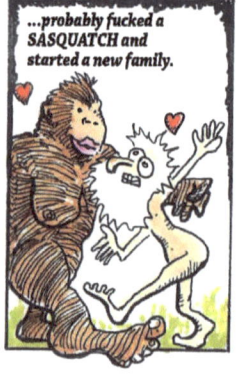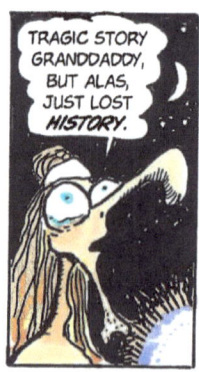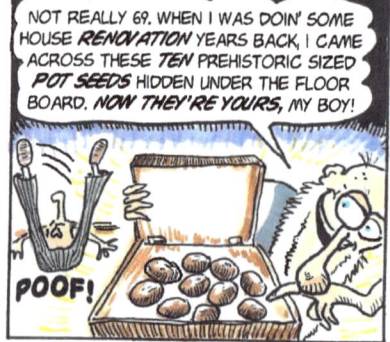

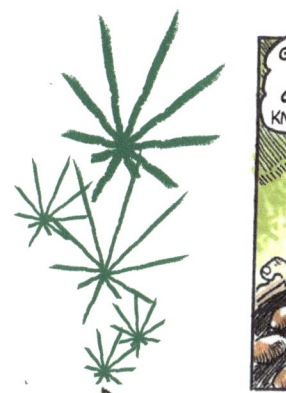
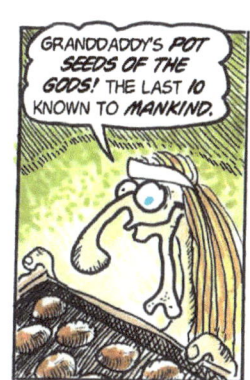
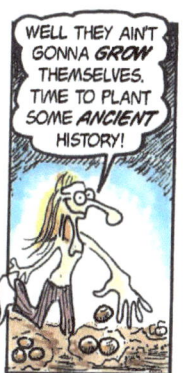
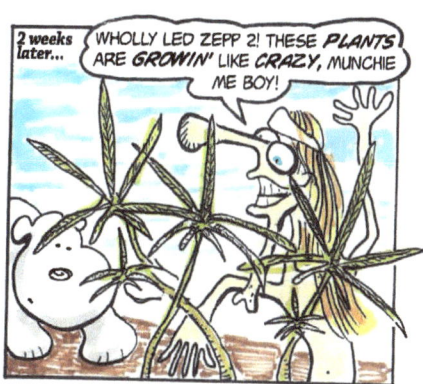
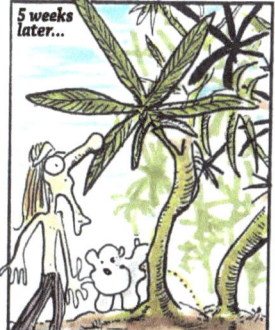
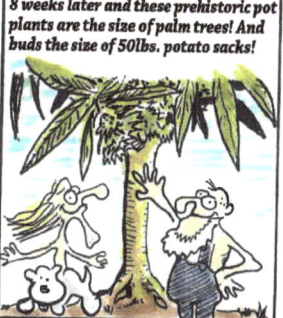
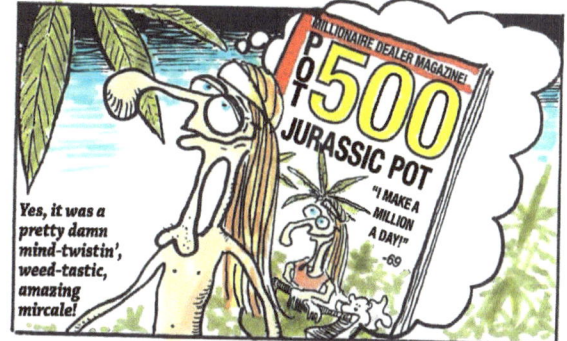
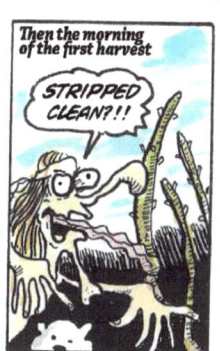
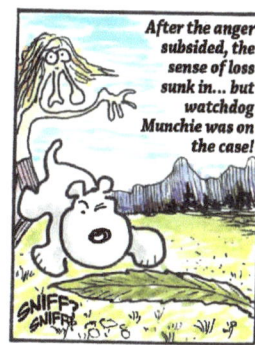
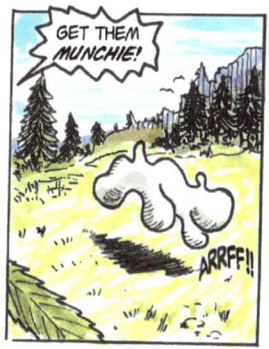
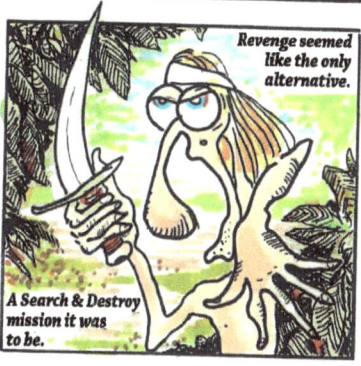
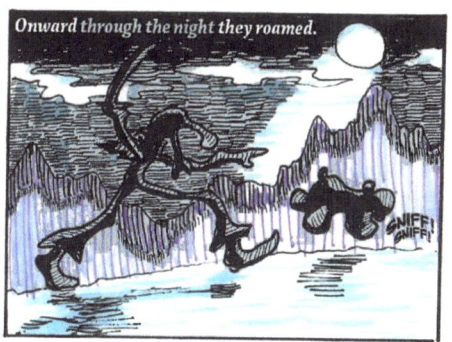
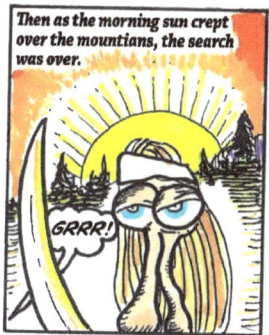
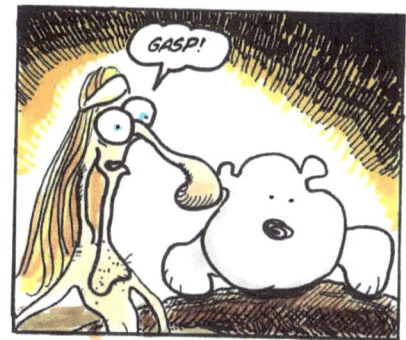
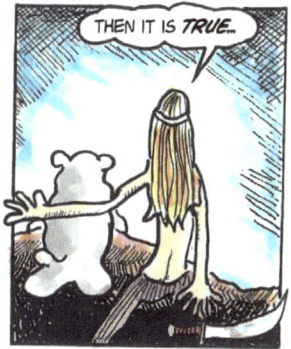
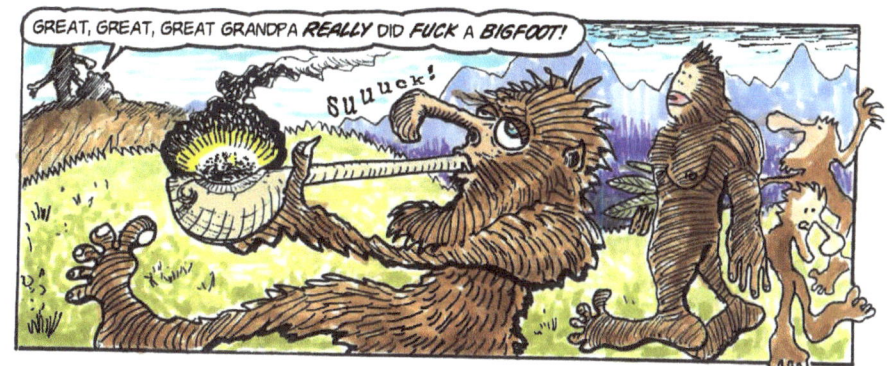

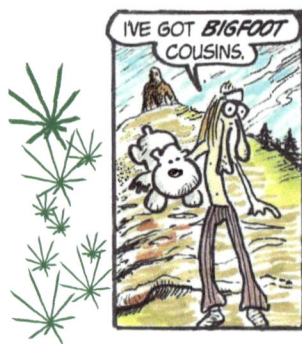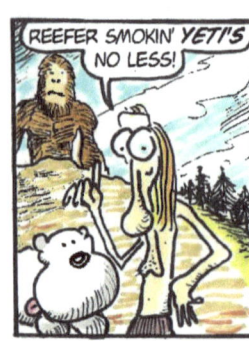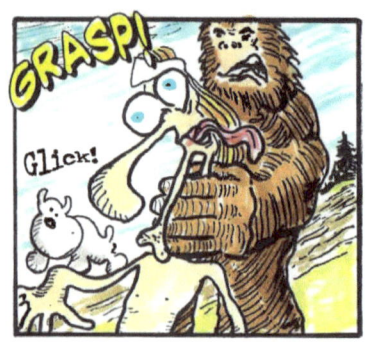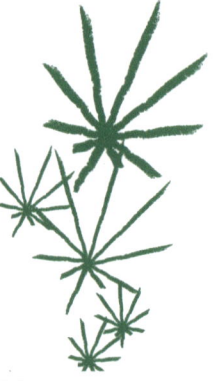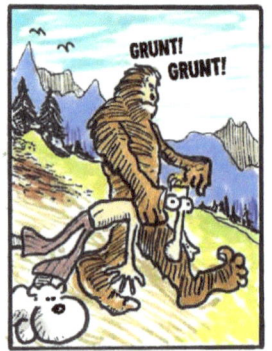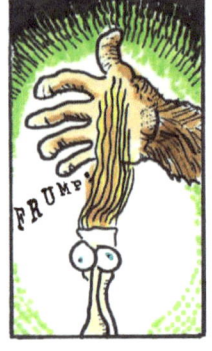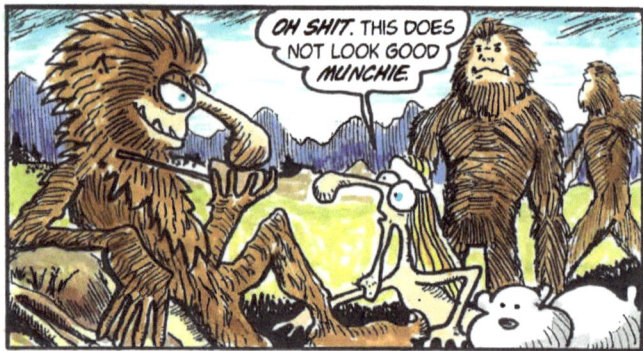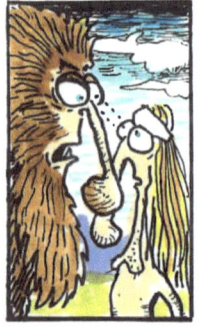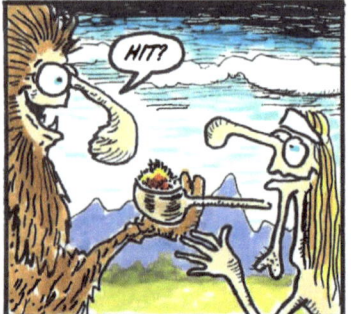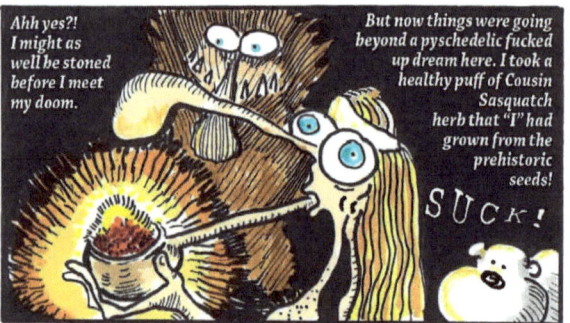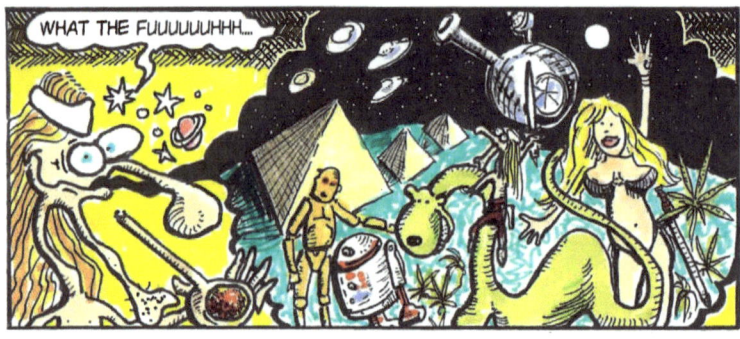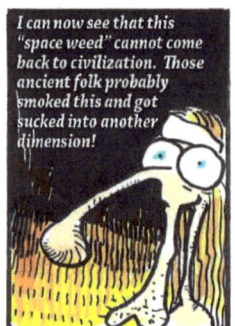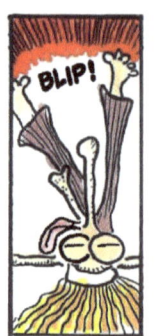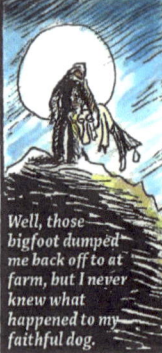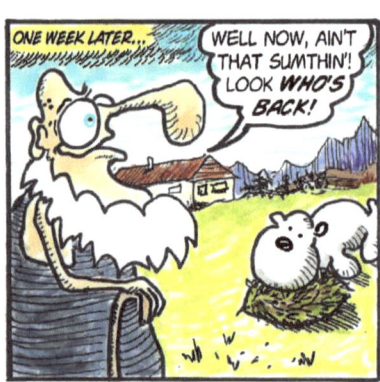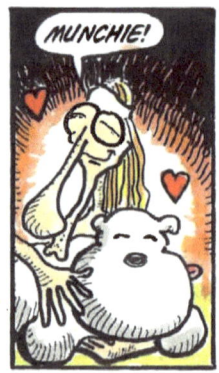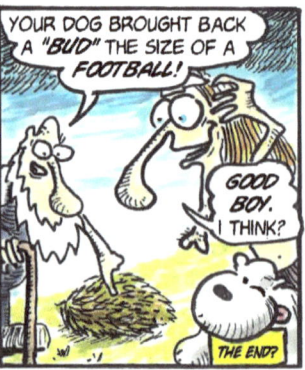

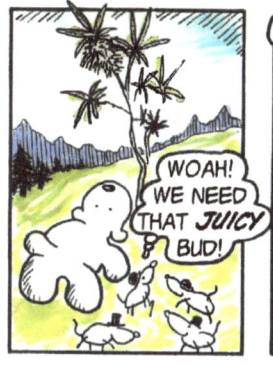
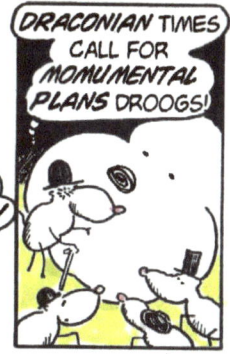
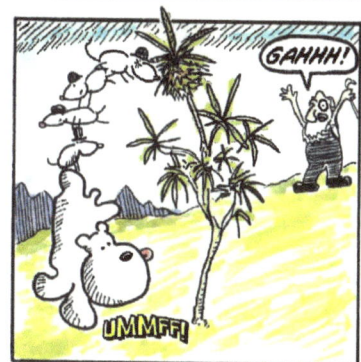
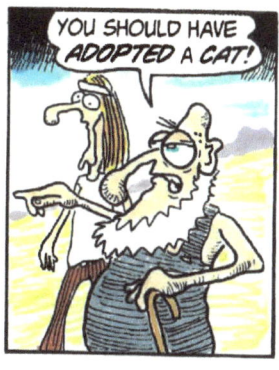
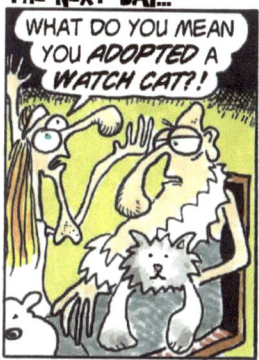
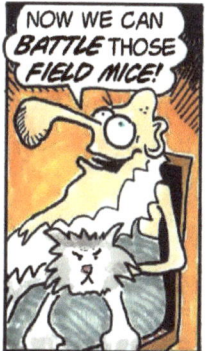
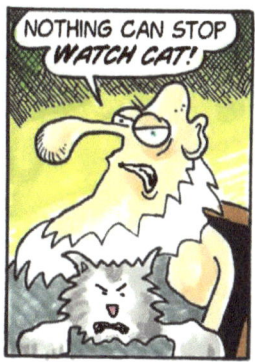
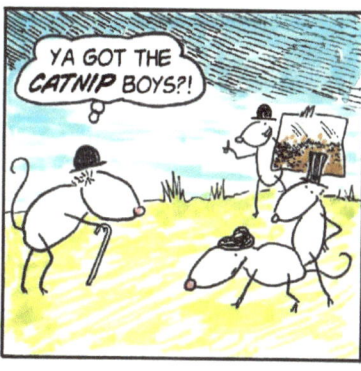
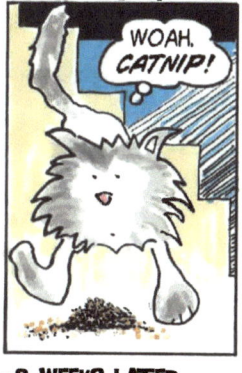
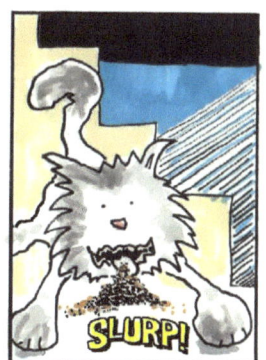
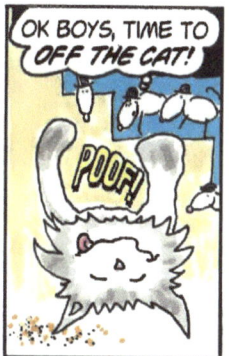
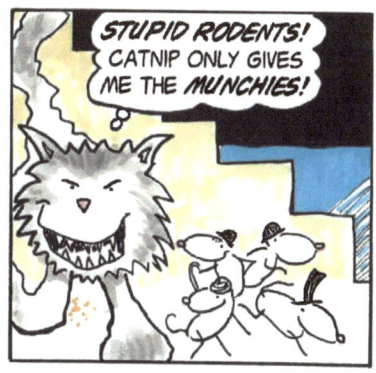
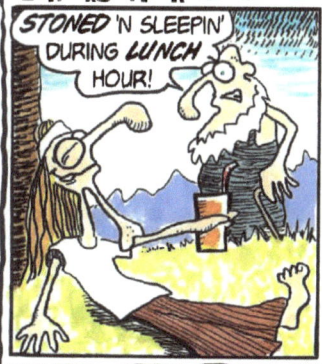
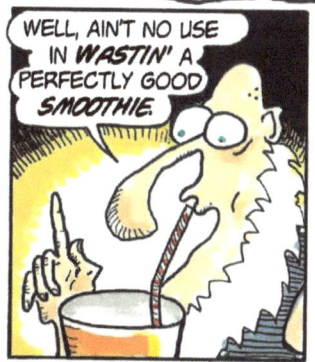
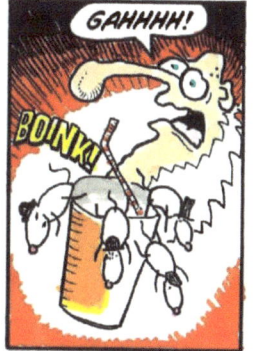
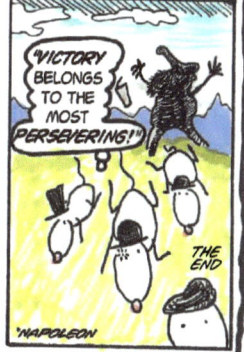

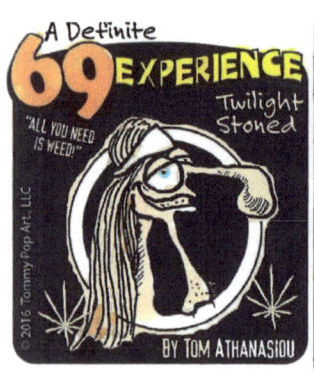
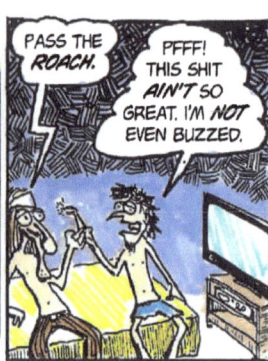
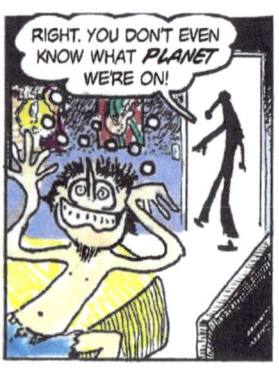
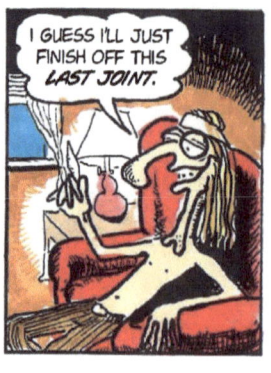
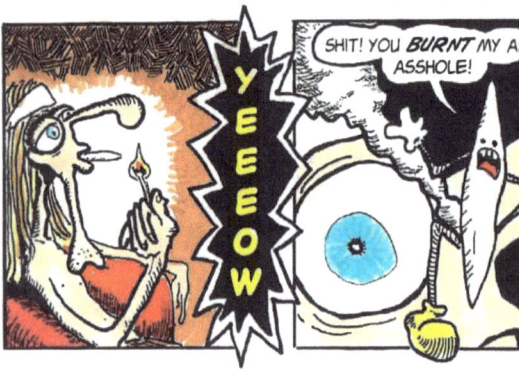
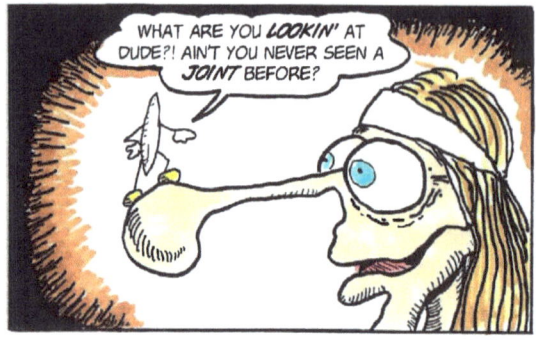
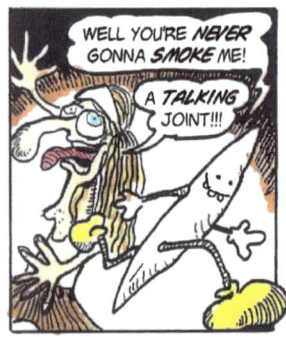
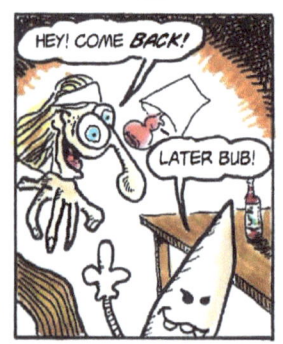
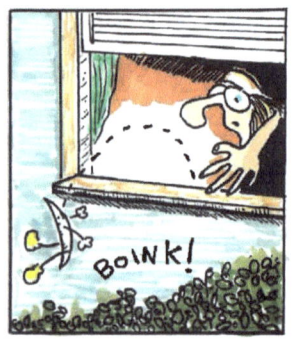
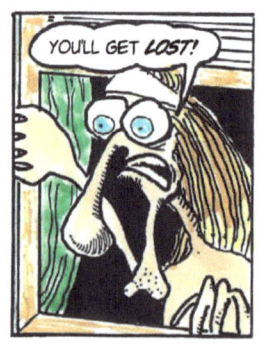
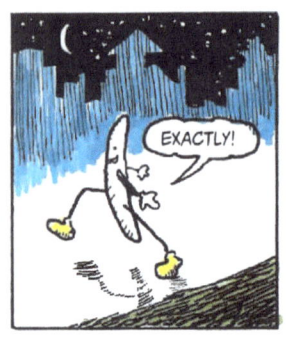
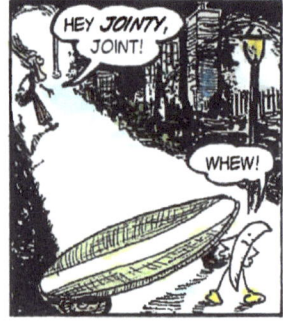
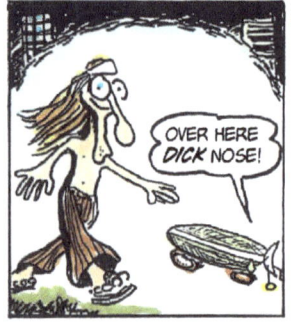
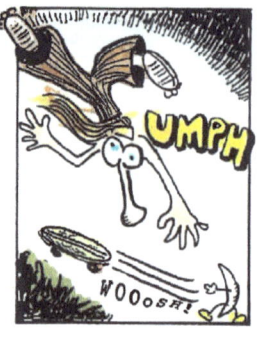
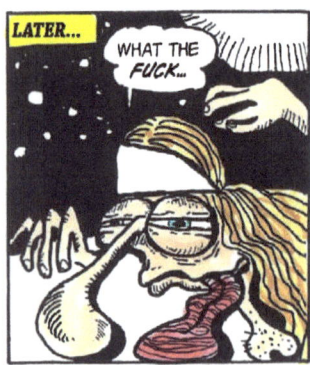
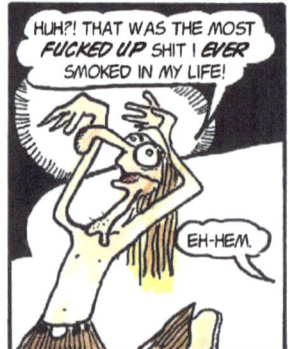
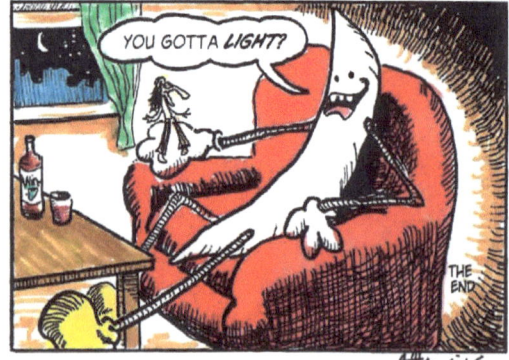

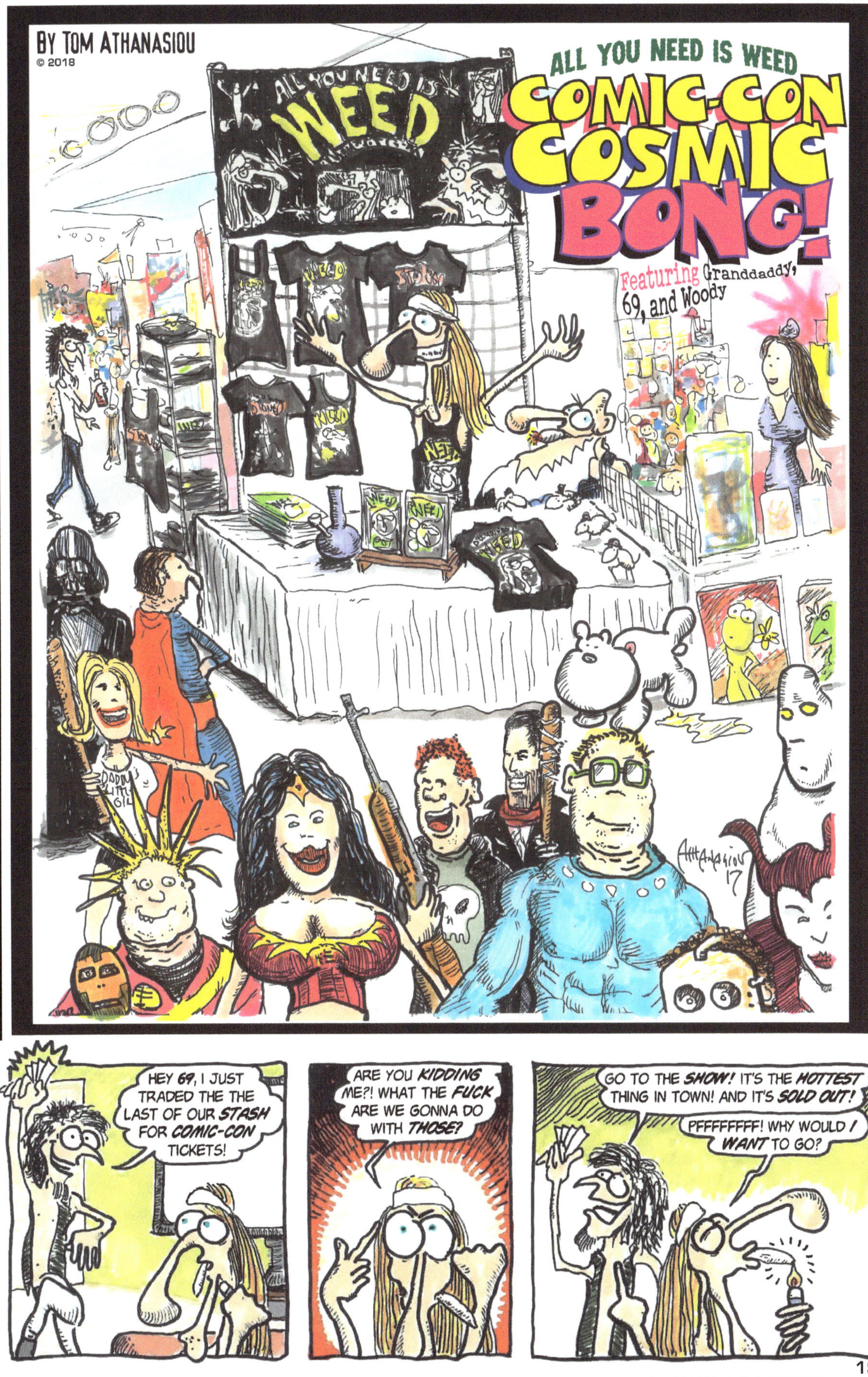

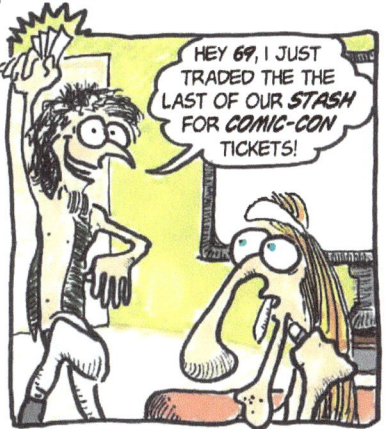
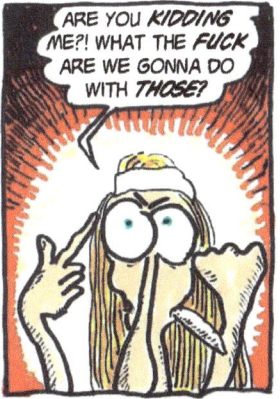
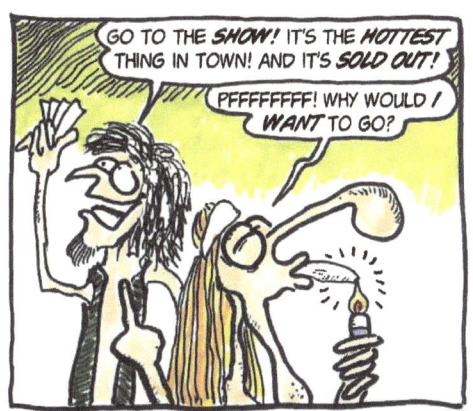

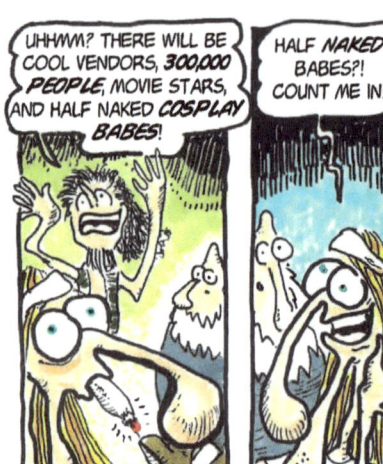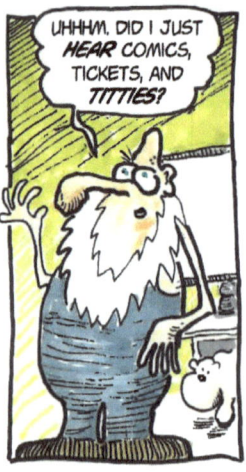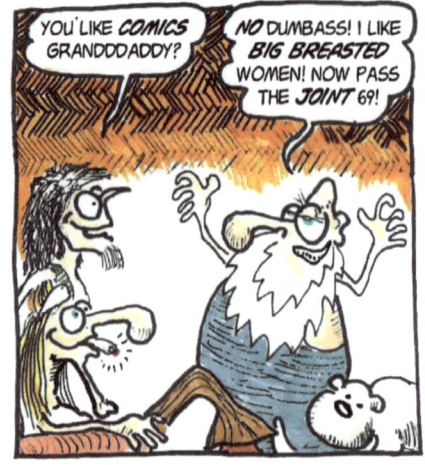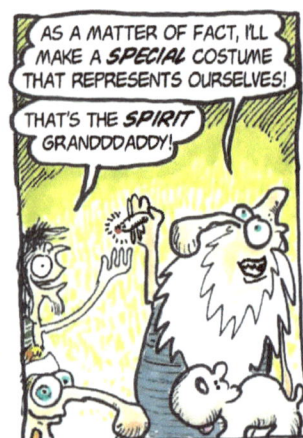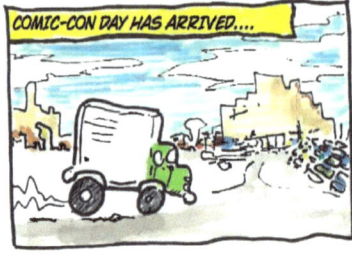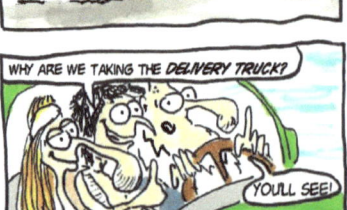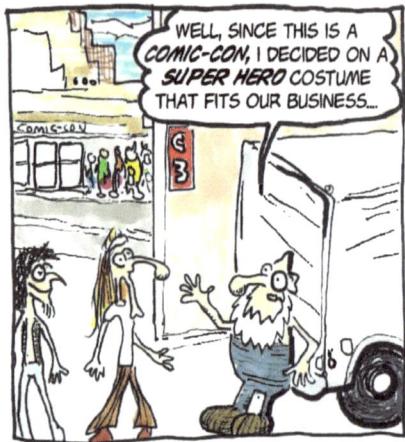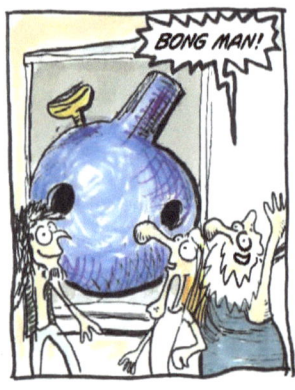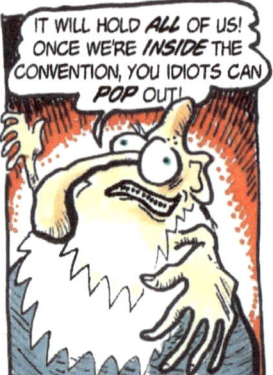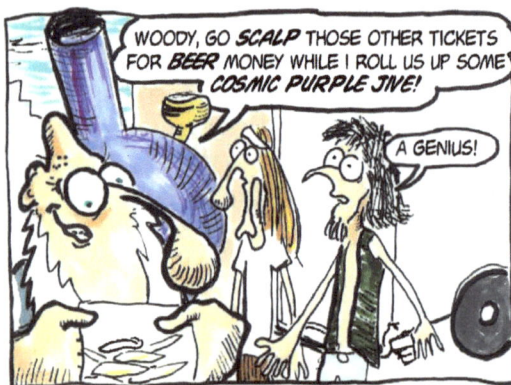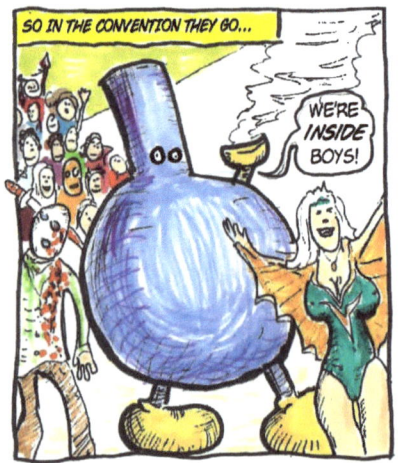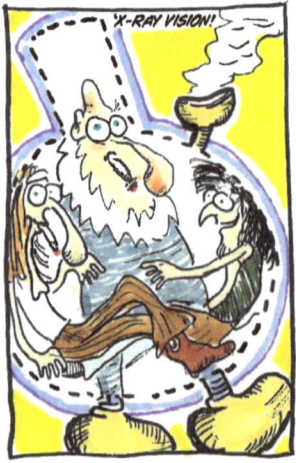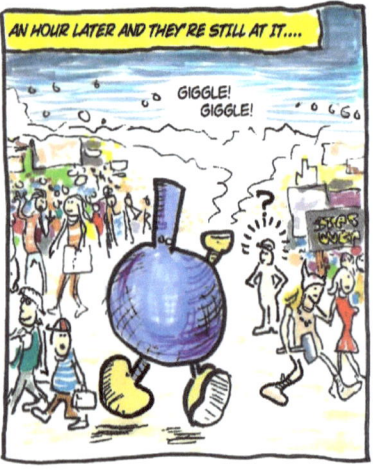

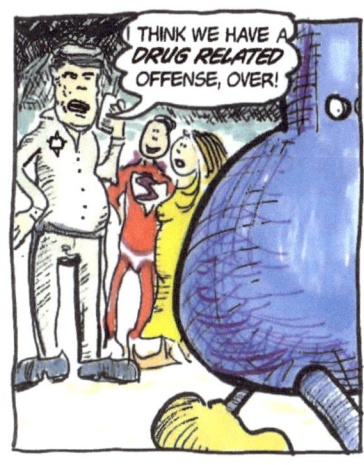
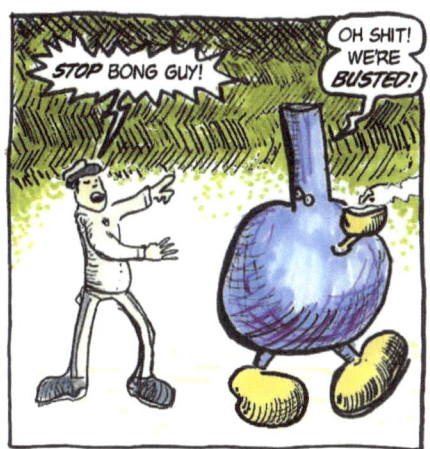
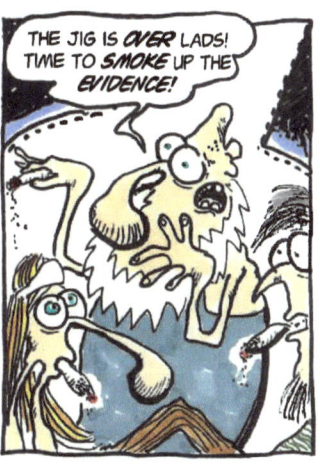
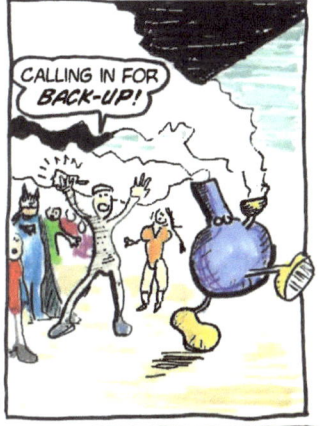
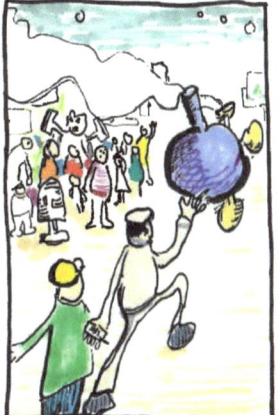
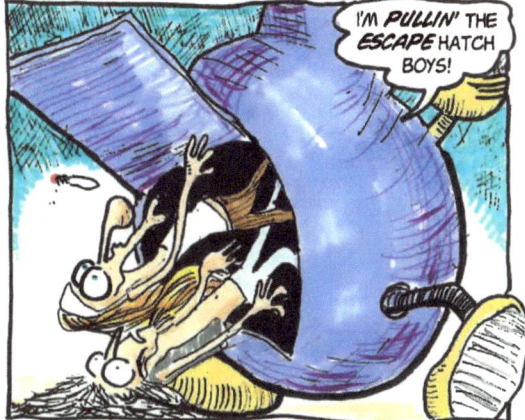
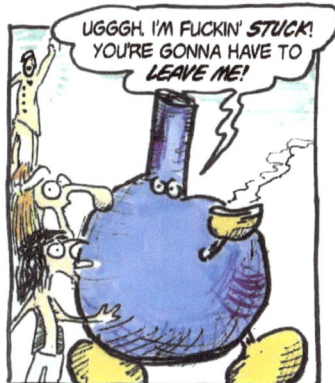
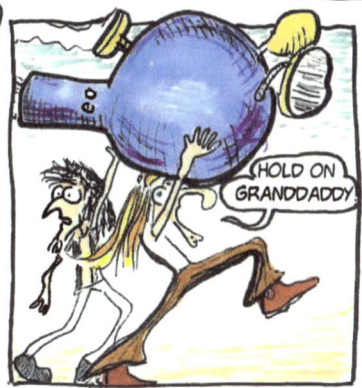
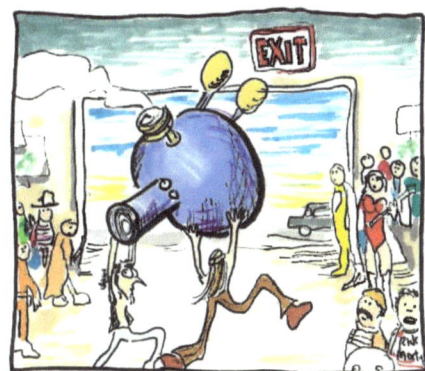
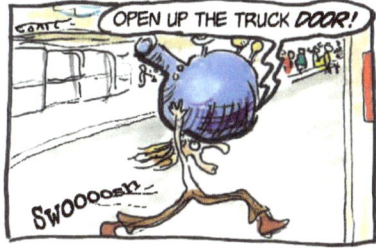
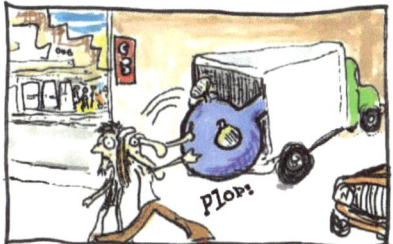
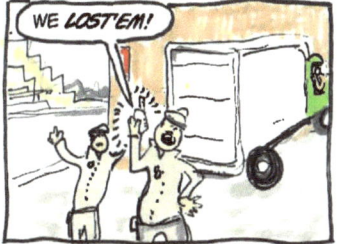
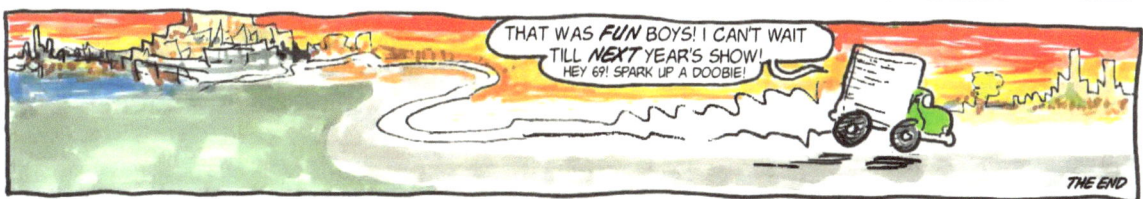

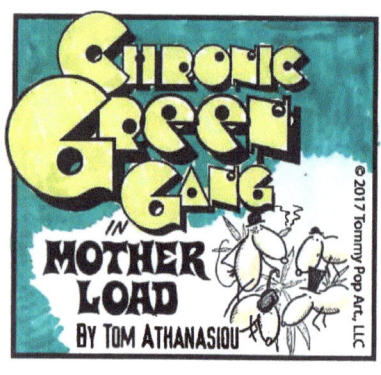
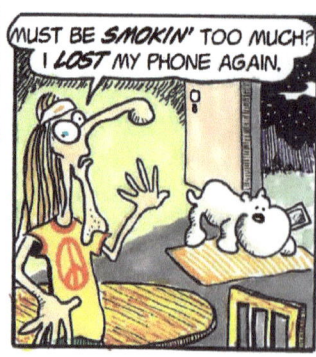
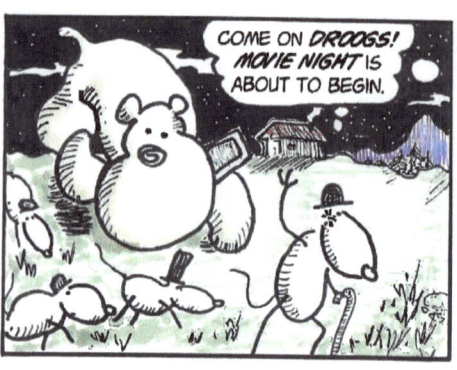
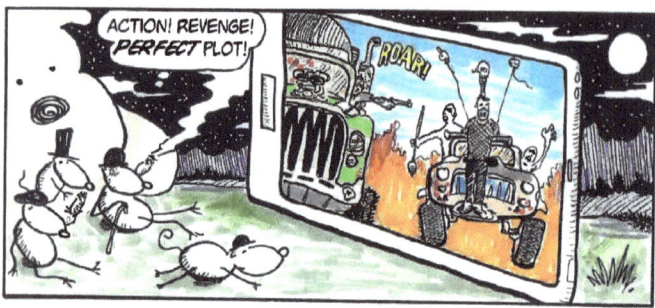
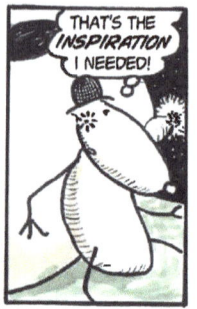
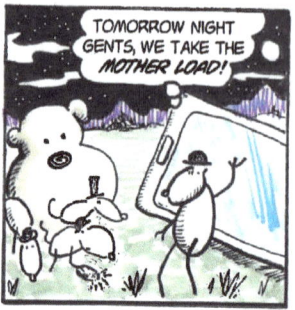
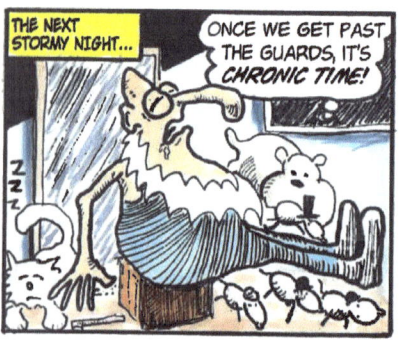
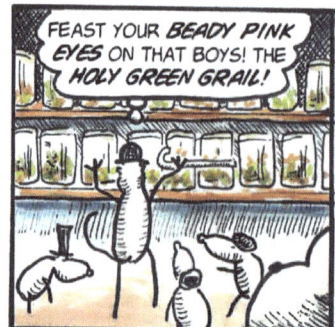
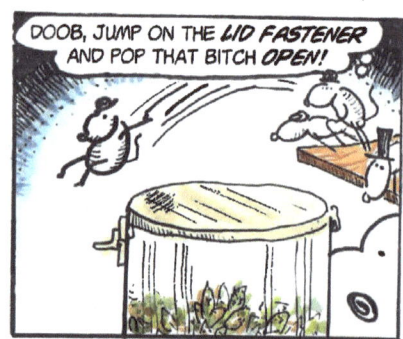
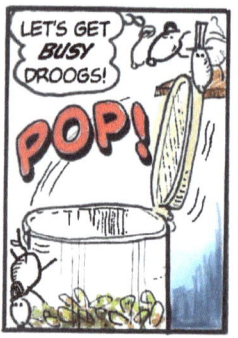
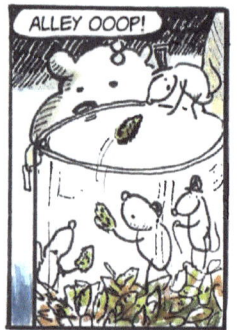
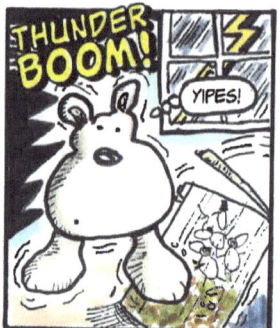
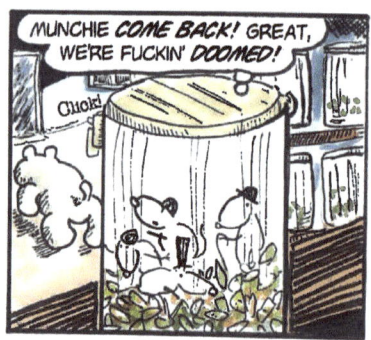
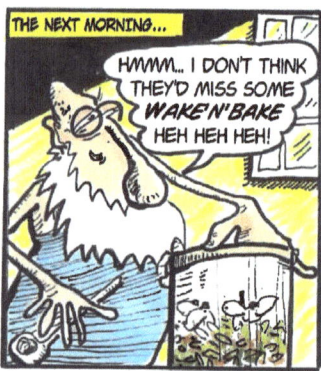
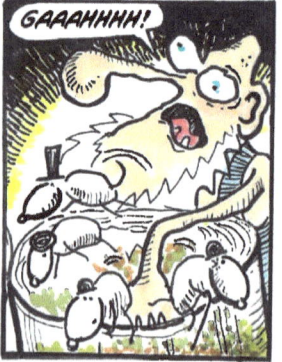
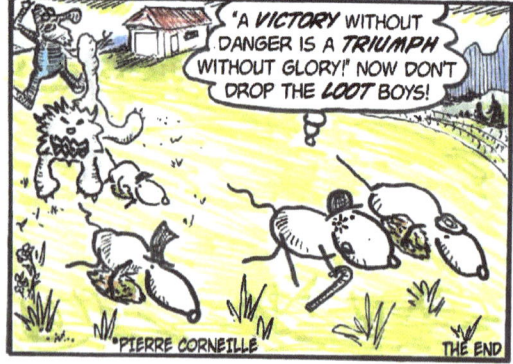

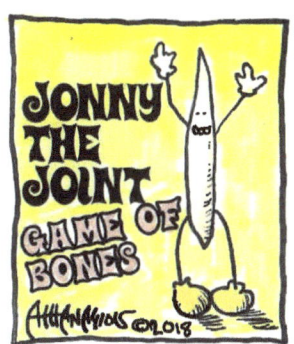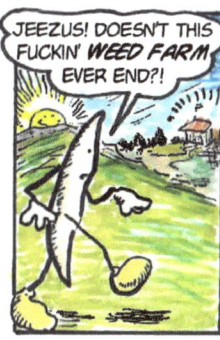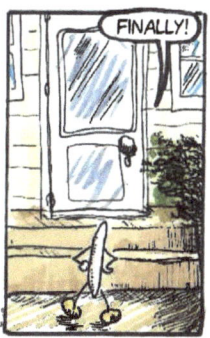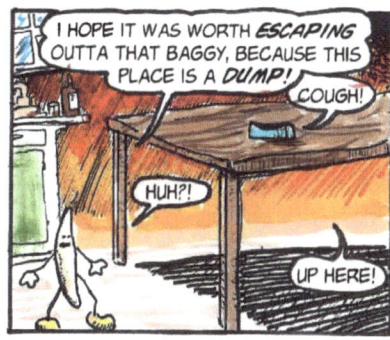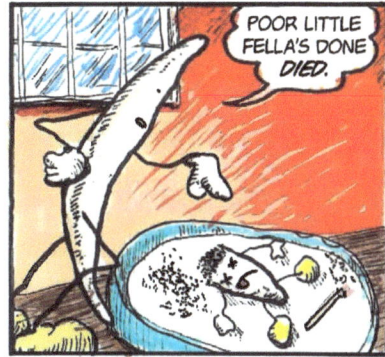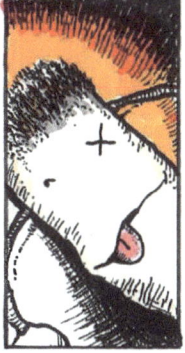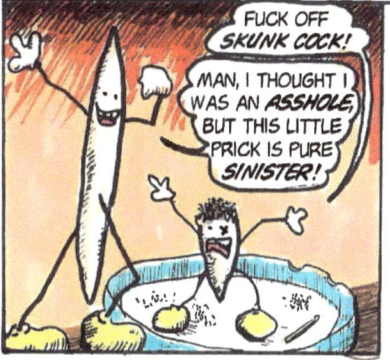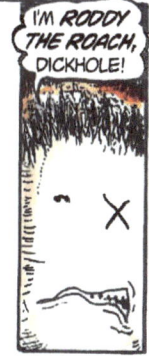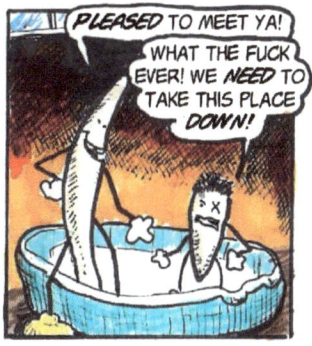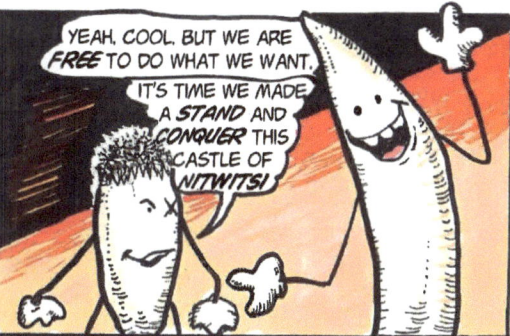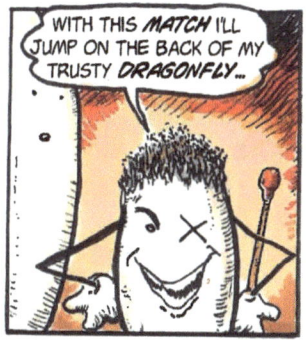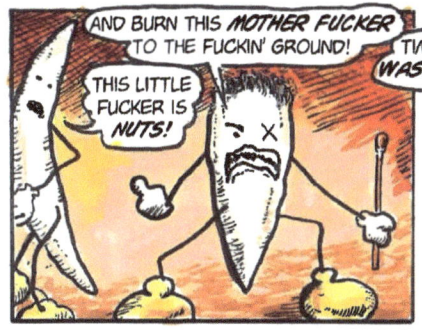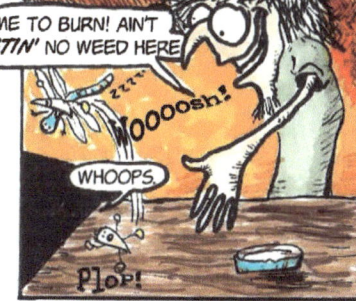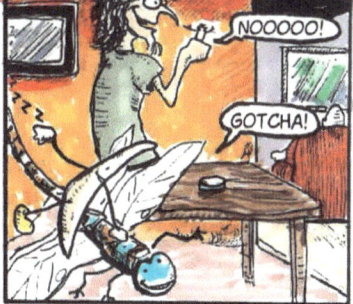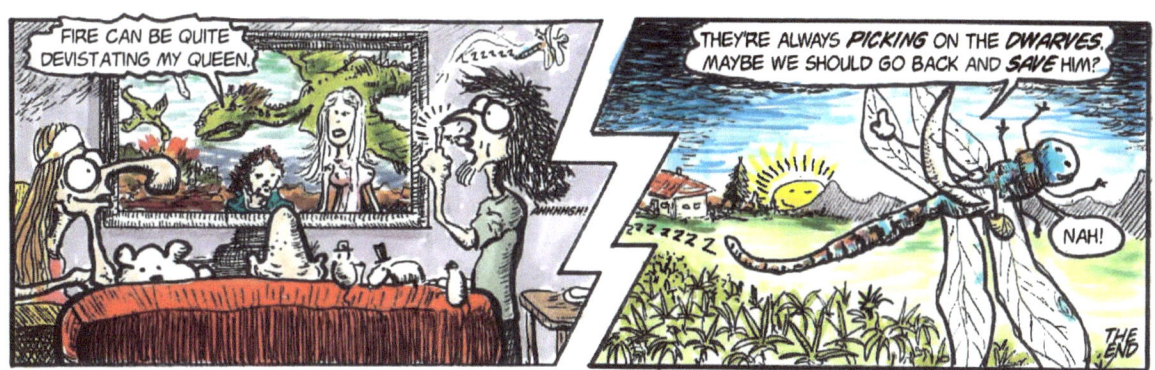

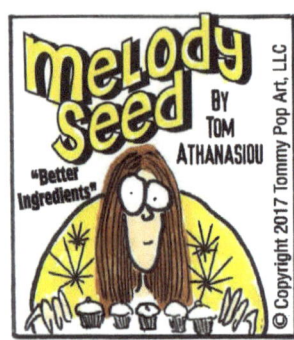
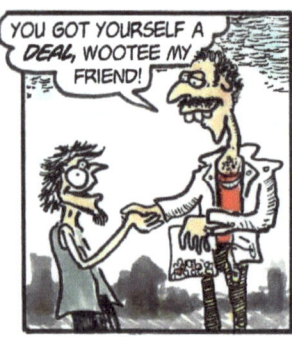
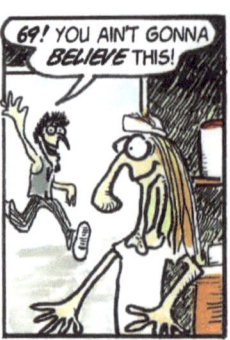
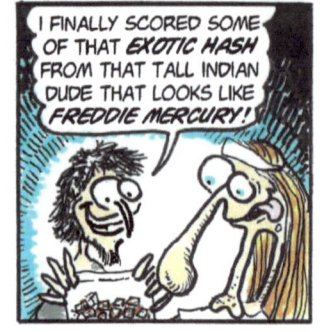
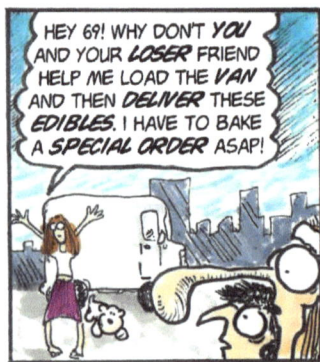
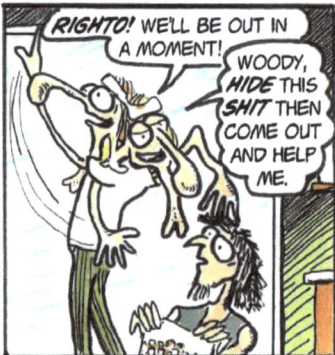
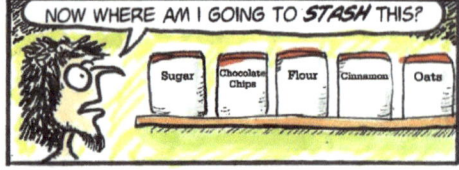
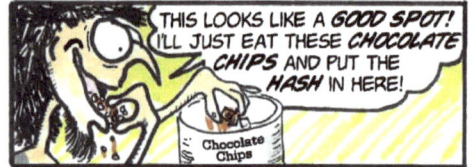
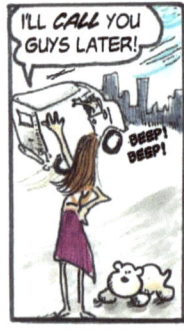
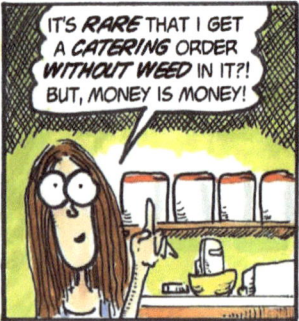
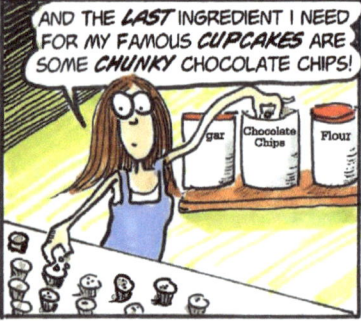
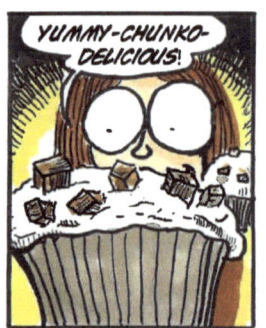
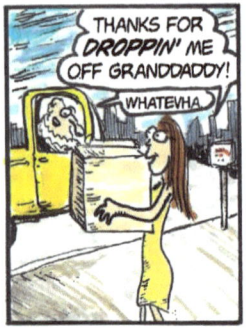
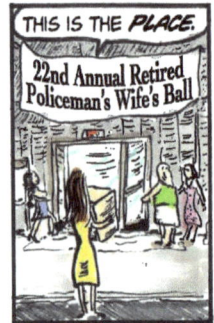
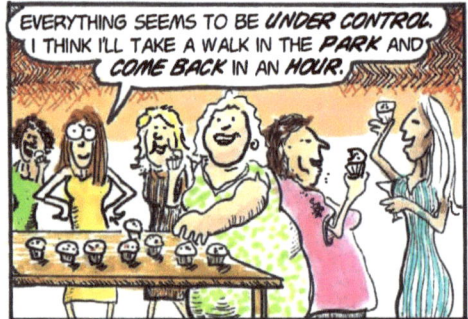
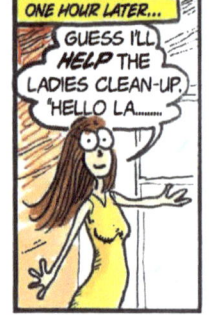
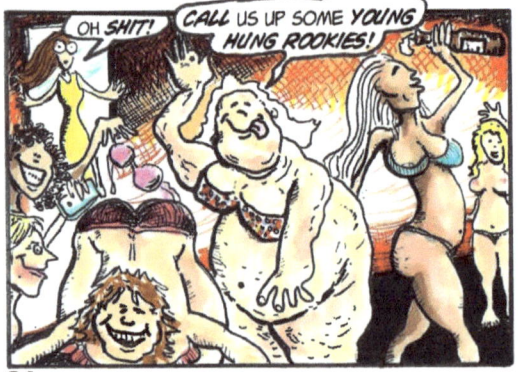
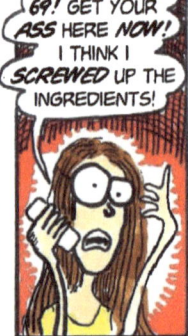
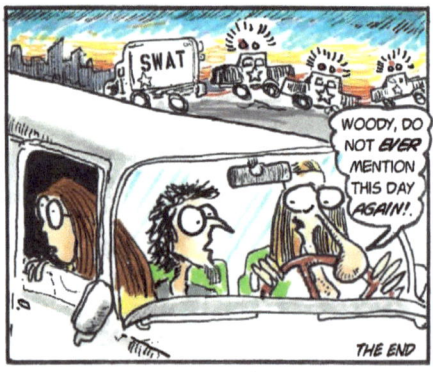

COMIC STRIPS

ALL YOU NEED IS WEED

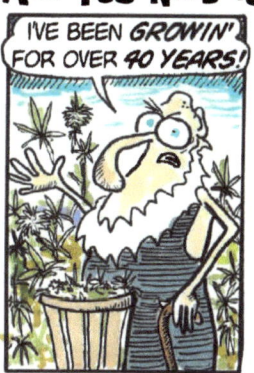
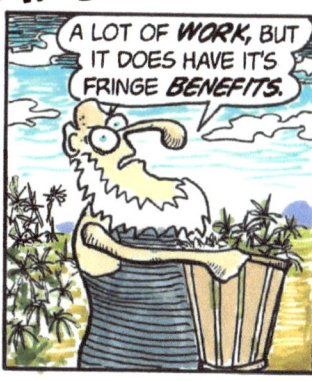
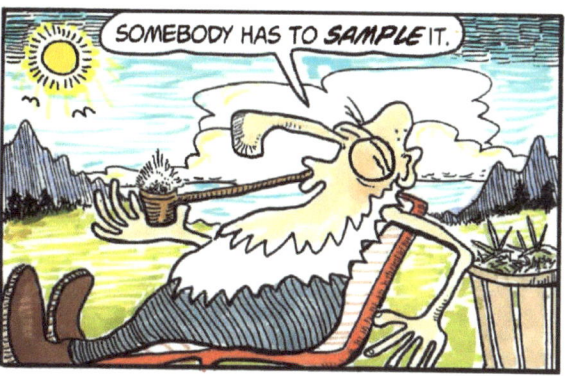

ALL YOU NEED IS WEED

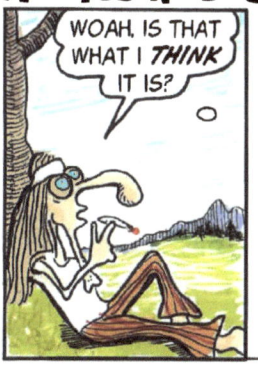
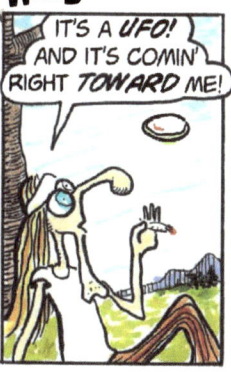
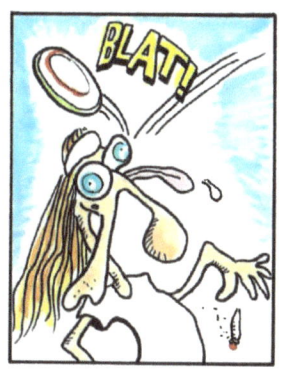
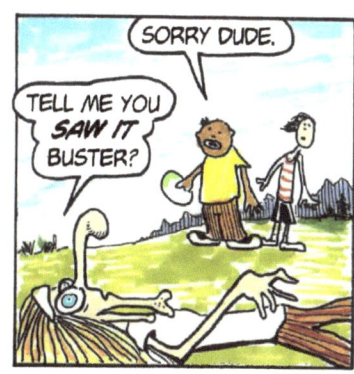

ALL YOU NEED IS WEED

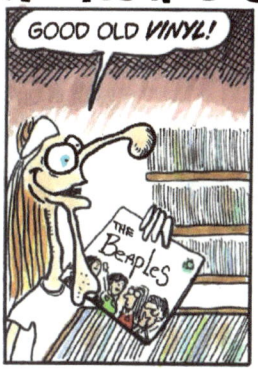
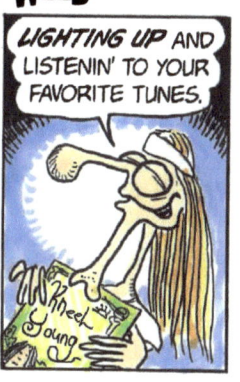
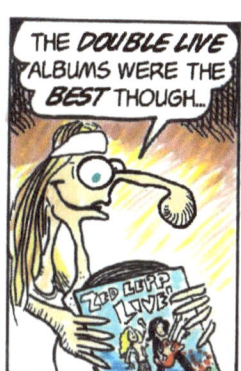
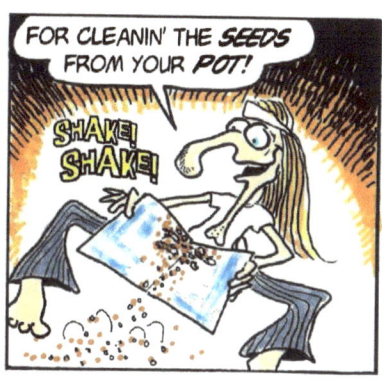

ALL YOU NEED IS WEED

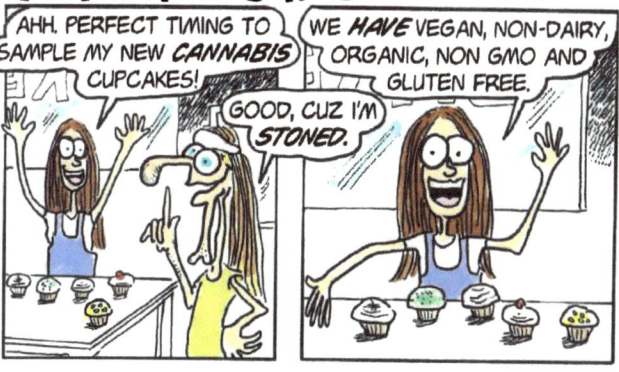
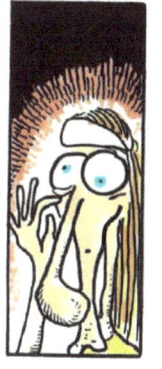
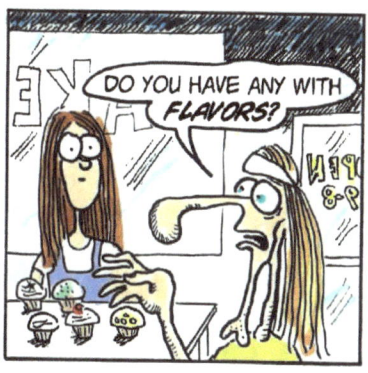

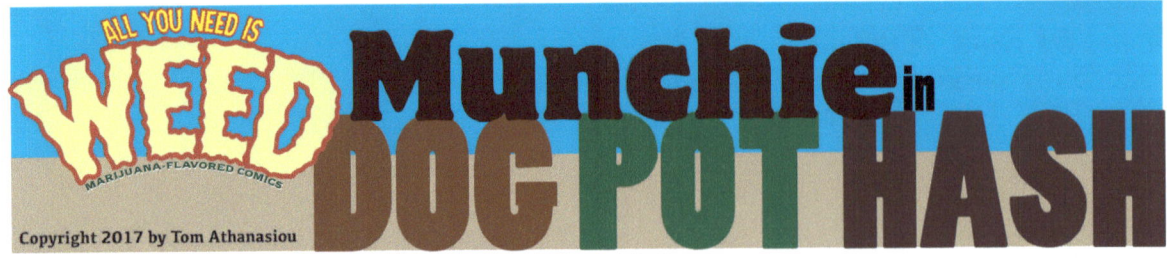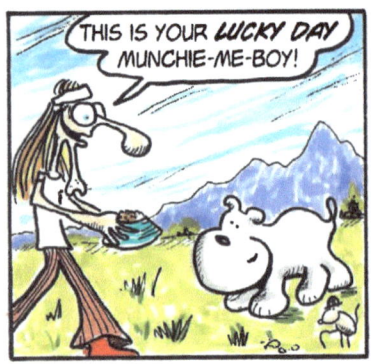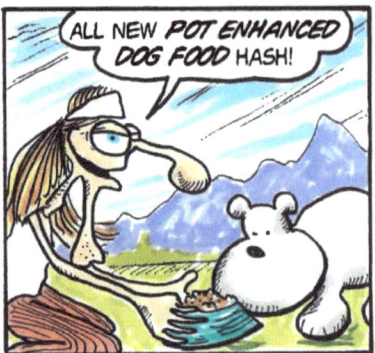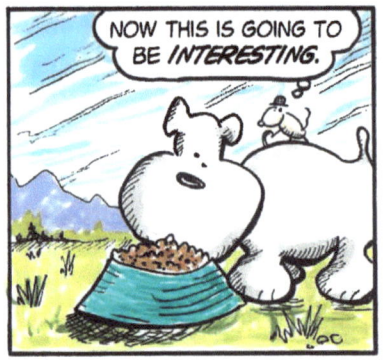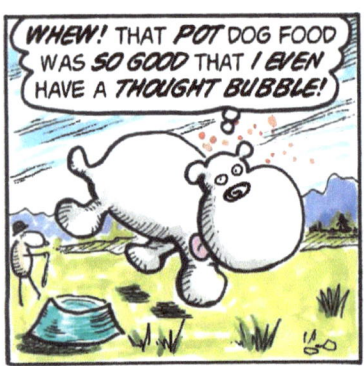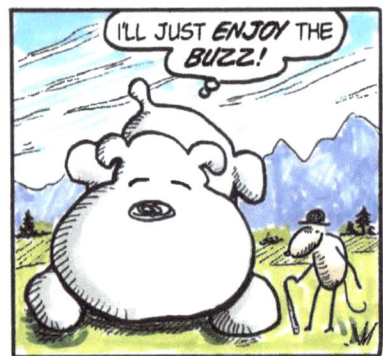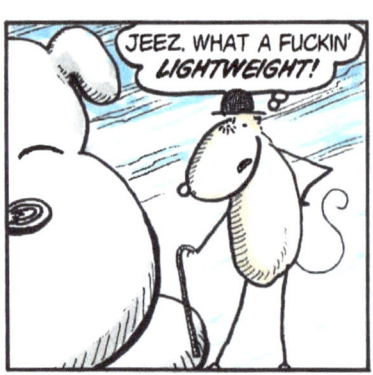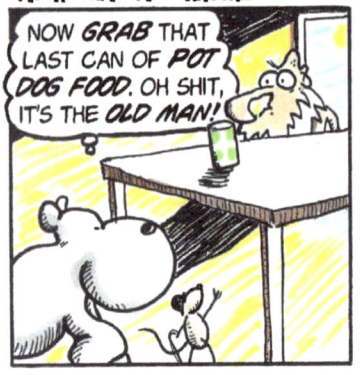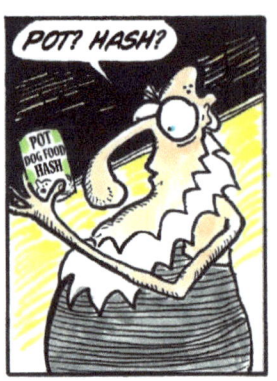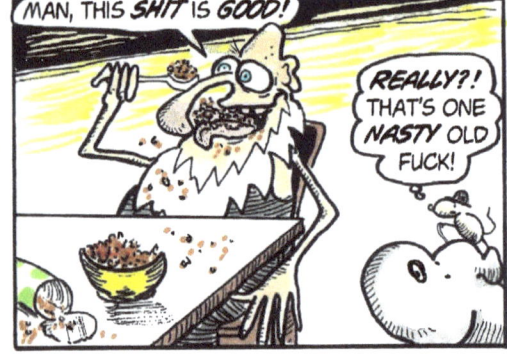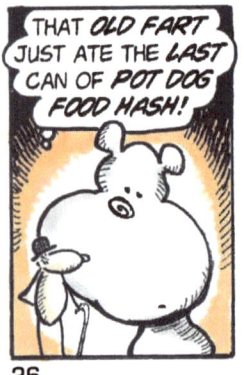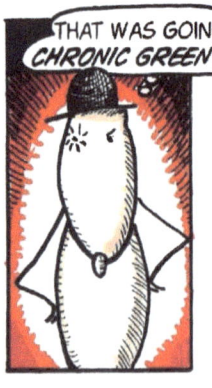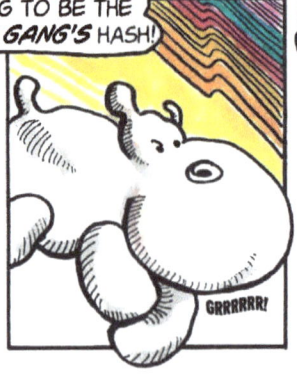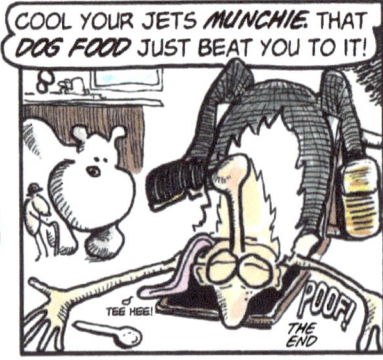

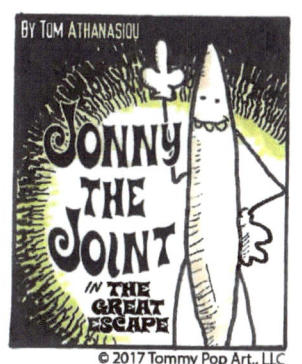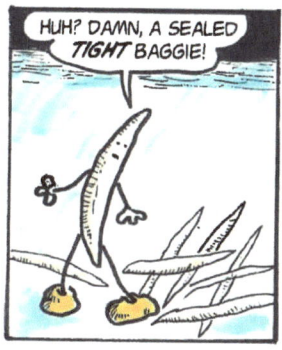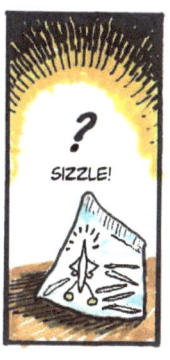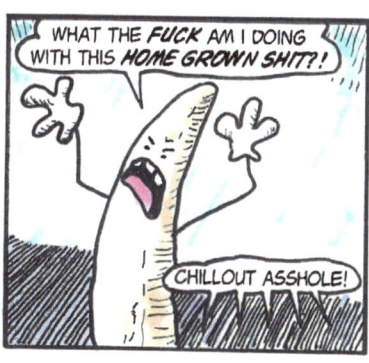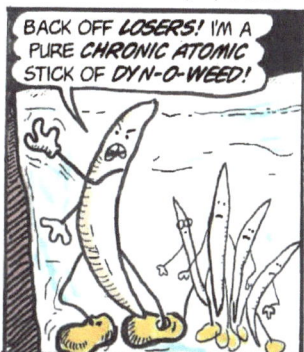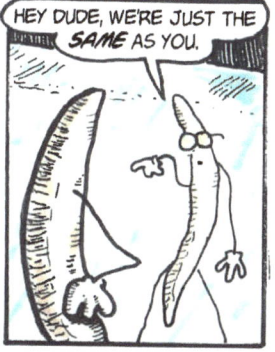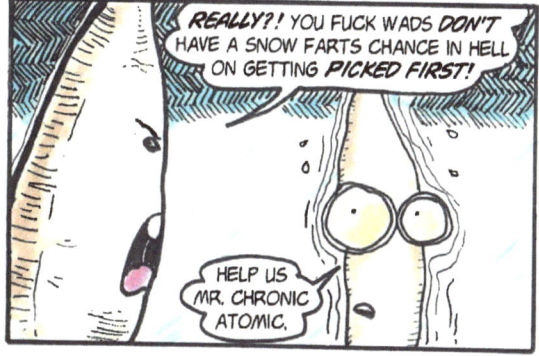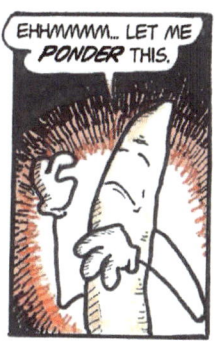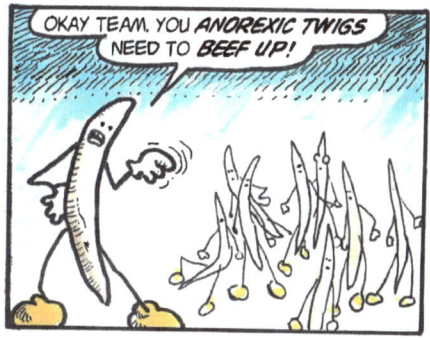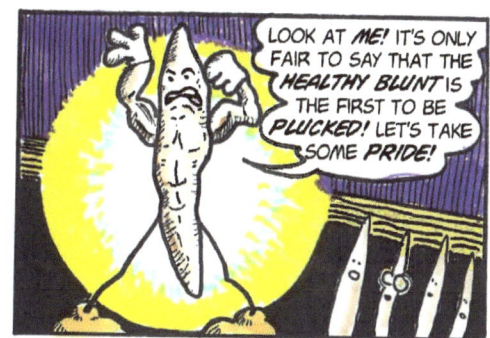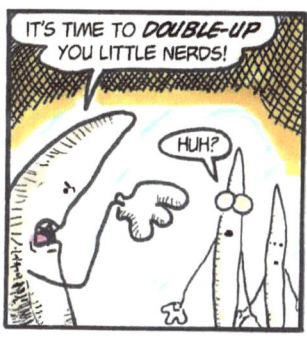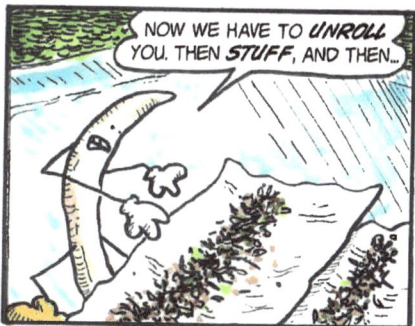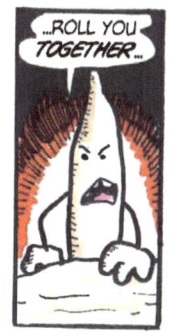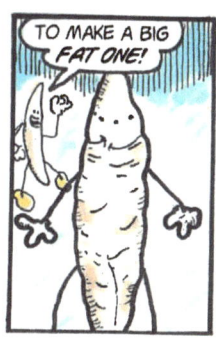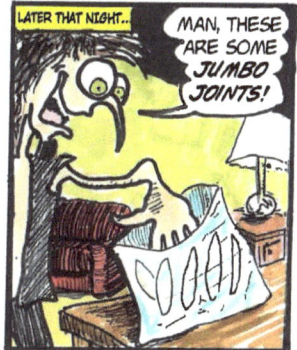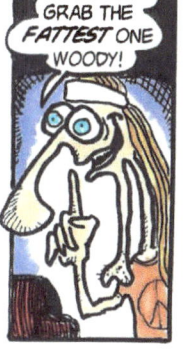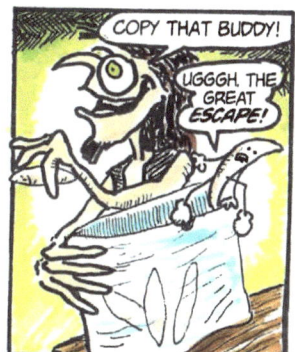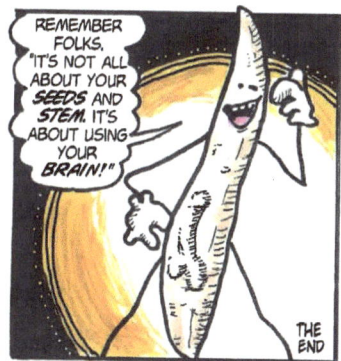

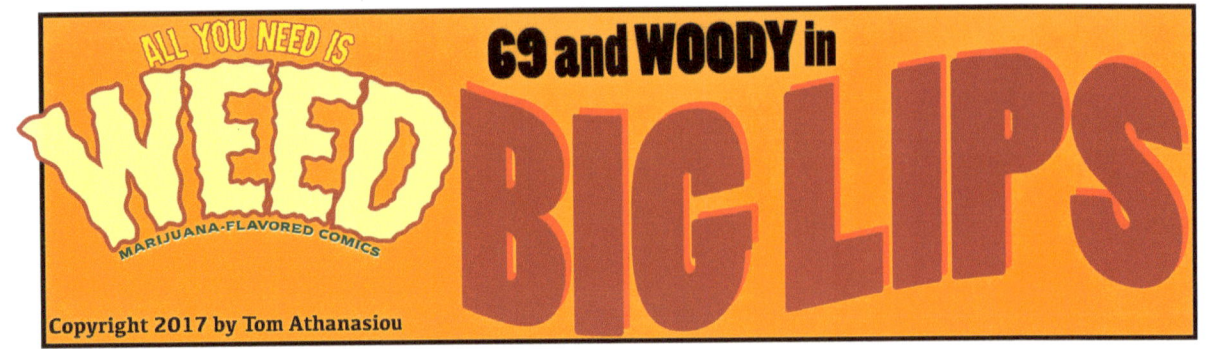
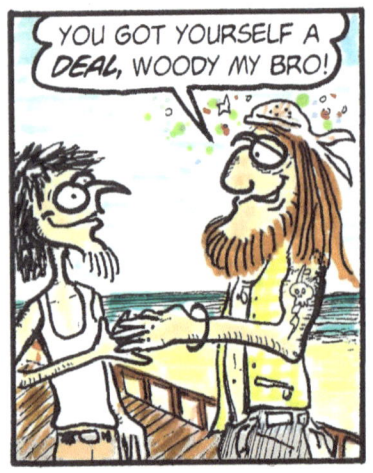
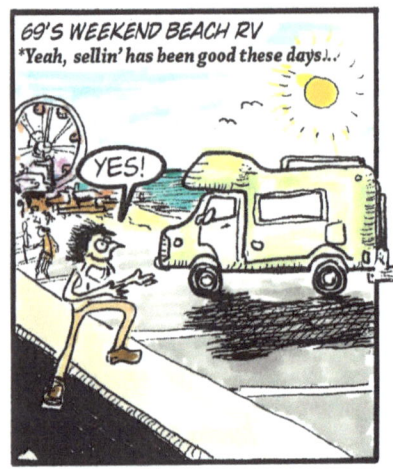
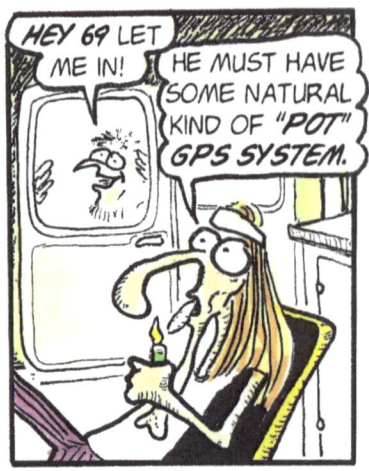
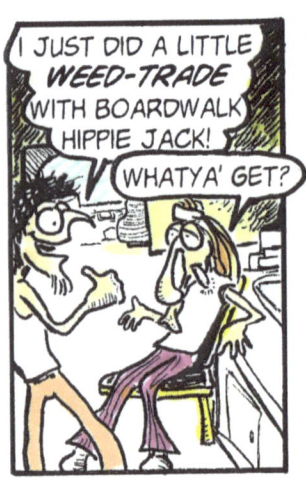
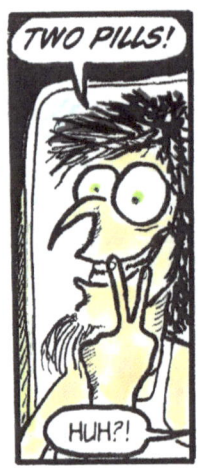
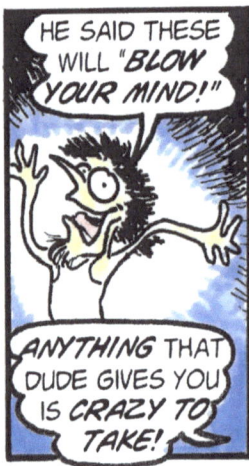
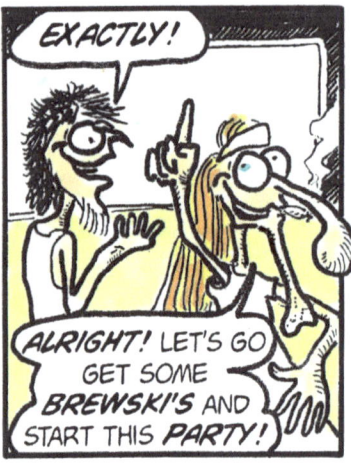
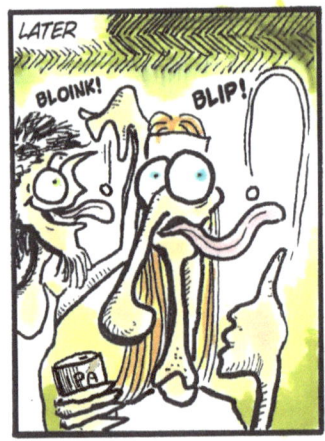
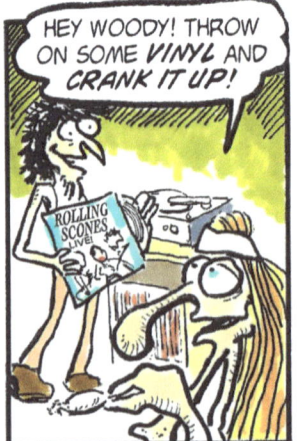
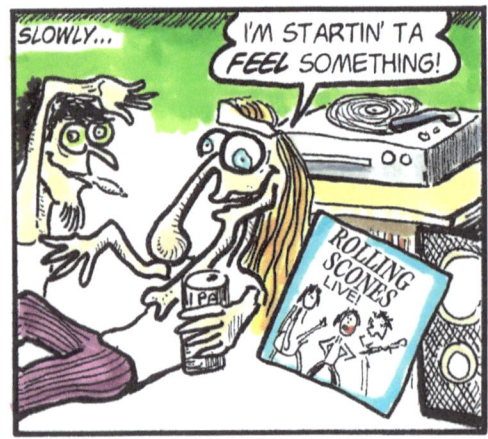

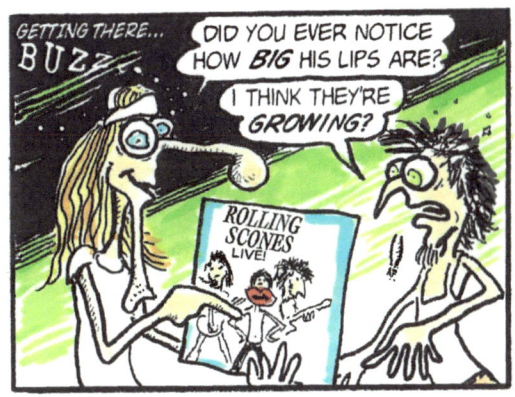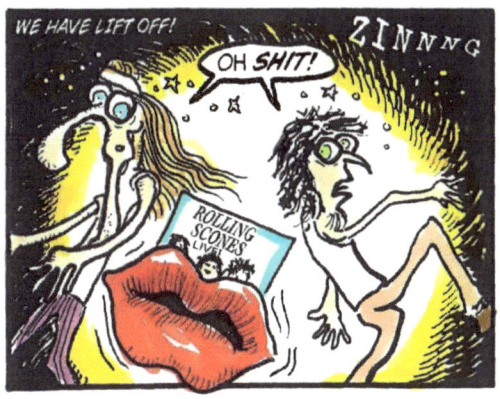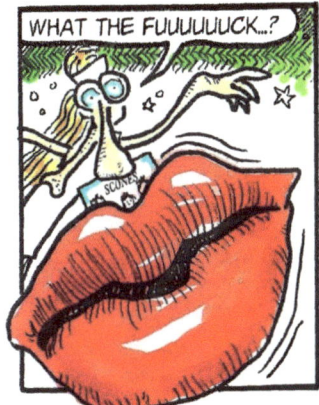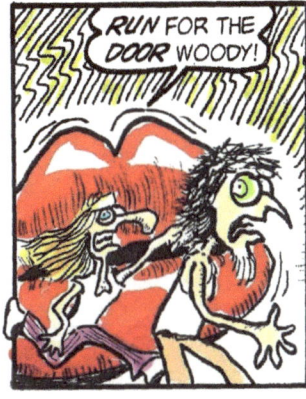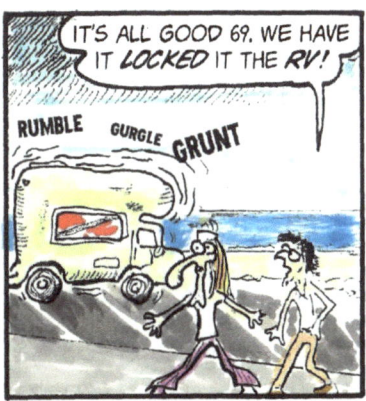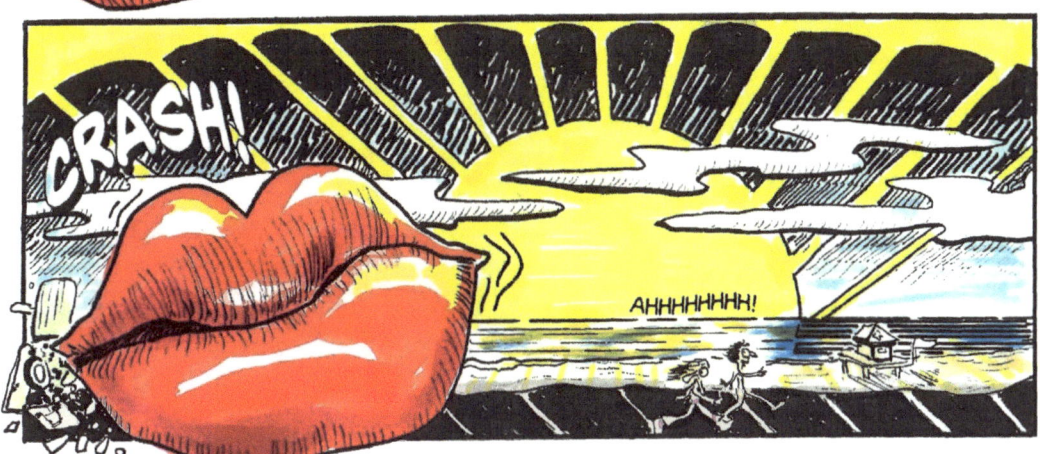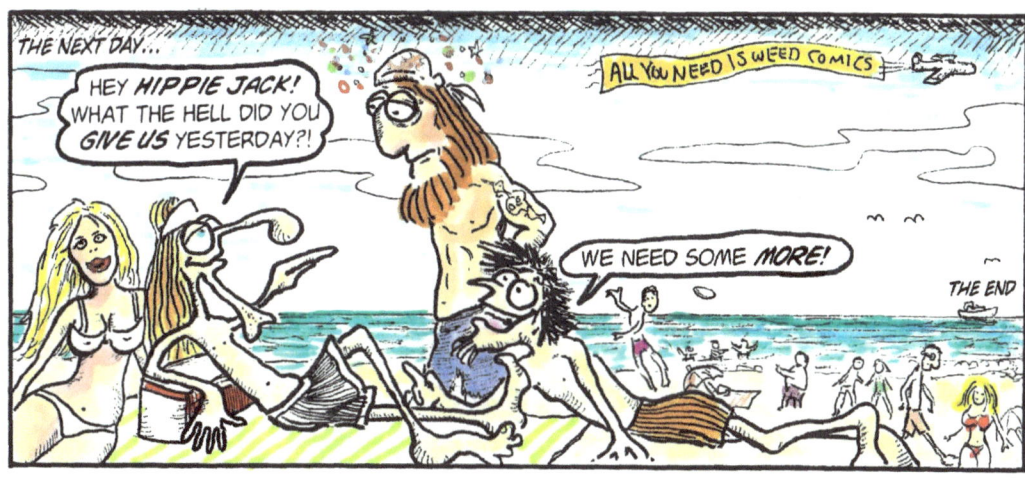

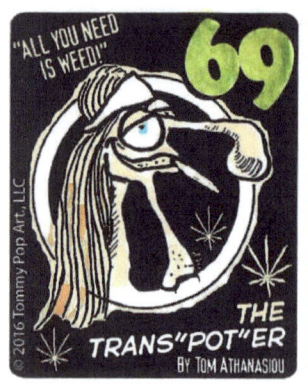
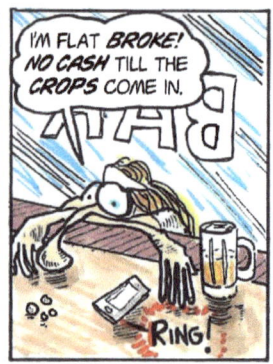
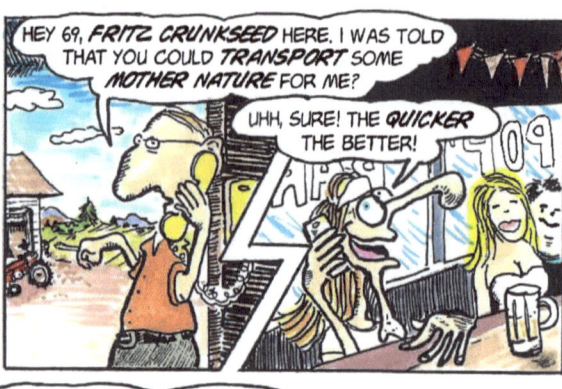
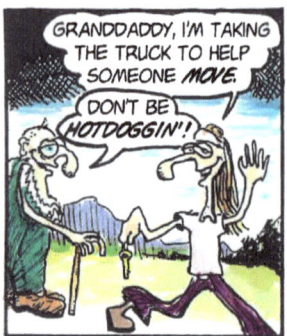
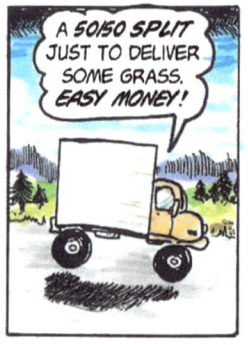
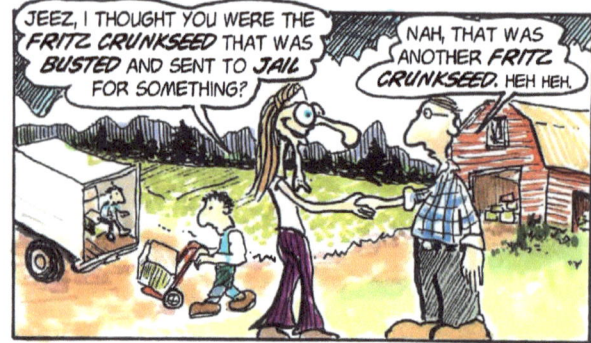
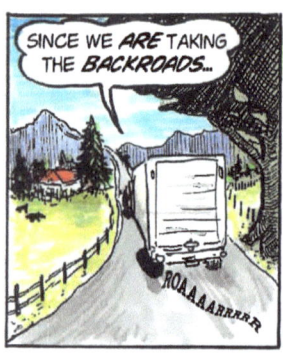
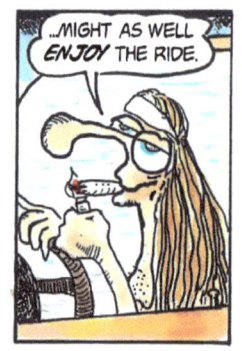
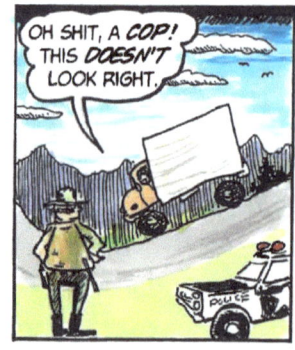
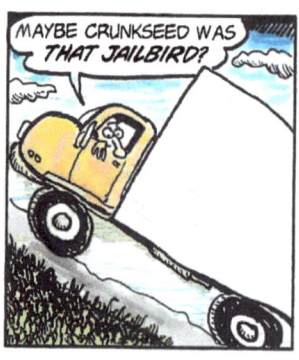
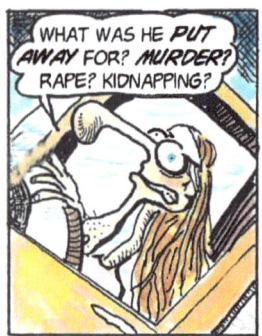
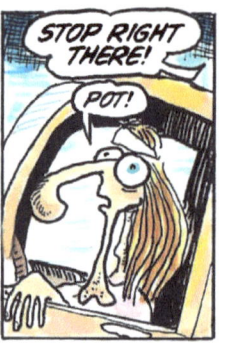
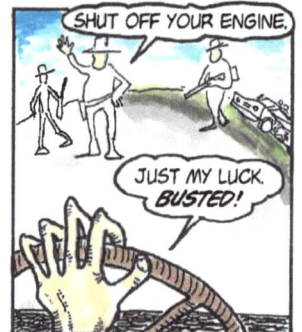
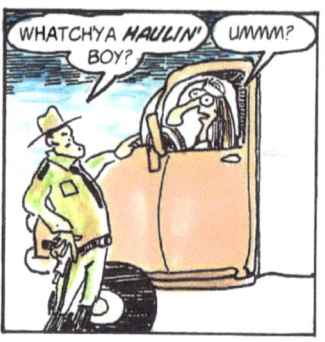
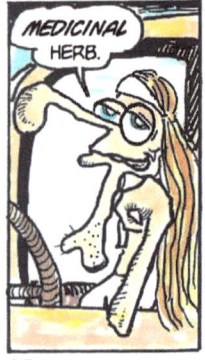
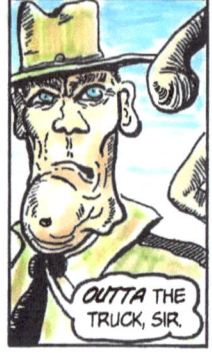
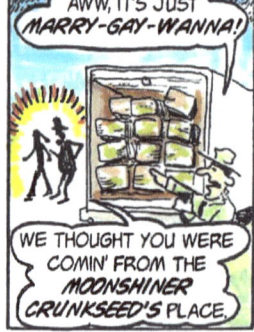
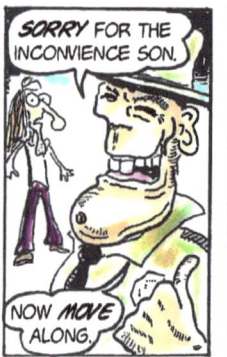
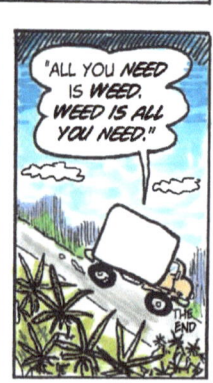

INTERVIEW ONE HITTER

ALL YOU NEED IS WEED
artist/writer Tom Athanasiou dips into the need for weed underground comix for a new generation

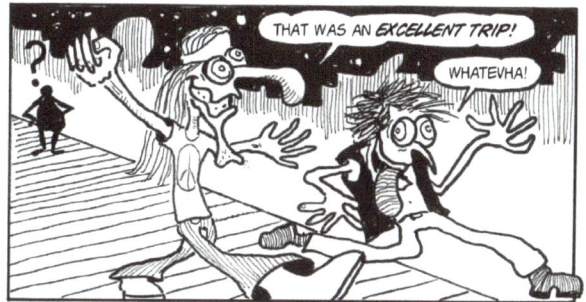

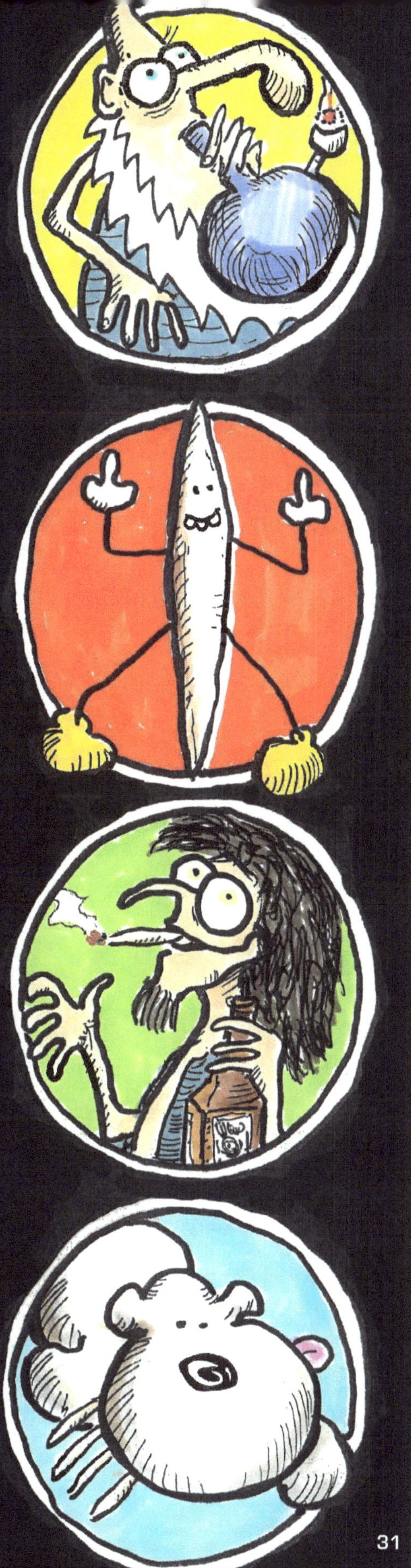

Q: Has it really been over 40 years since you created the character "69"?

T.A: Yep. I started these comics in 1976 when I was a child. He was the first character in my new reefer found world.

Why did you decide, 40 some years later, to do an underground comix series with these "totally 70's" reefer-smoking characters?

I believe that everything always comes back full-circle. Meaning that these underground comix were extremely popular back in the day, and I feel that they can be brought to life again in the mainstream for this new surrealistic pot generation.

When did you begin creating these comics?

Get ready for the long history story, folks. These underground comix were total taboo to a little kid like me who had discovered this in a school library book, of all things — *Comix: A History of Comic Books in America* by Les Daniels & Mad Peck Studios. And the second book that really hit on the taboo part was a public library gem, *The History Of Underground Comics* by Mark James Estren which was the book that blew my mind with all its titillating content that was definitely not inside *MAD Magazine*, *Cracked*, or any *Marvel/DC* comic. Intriuged by the dope factor, I saved up enough money to purchase the ultimate druggie bible at the local mall, *High Times Encyclopedia Of Recreational Drugs* where I was immediately hooked to the works of my two favorite underground comix artists, Robert Crumb and Gilbert Shelton. They were the main cartoonists of this book and were the same two who had grasped my attention in the library books. Shelton's *The Fabulous Furry Freak Brothers* spoke to me, and Crumb was a whole new insane anything goes way of creating comic art! The true master creator of this underground comix world. I am still mesmerized by Crumb's talent and output of art work.

So I'm around 13 years old and I started doing my own little strips and characters, which turned into the one-page stories like the many underground comix books I had started to collect. I had built a drawing desk and started cranking out these dope comix of my own. Lots of 'em! That was my obsession. But I got older, times had changed, and the whole hippie stoner thing evolved into a sex, drugs, and rock'n'roll thing. Off to art college I went, and got into oil painting, illustration, and eventually became a successful commercial artist. And here I am now 40 years later, going back to what I know and love, which are creating these anything-goes, pot-influenced, one-paged stories.

Wouldn't it be cool to have your characters break into the mainstream?
Sure, that is every comic artist's intention. Now seems the perfect time to unveil these characters to a world that seems to be becoming more pot-friendly by the minute. We do, pun intended, have a budding audience. I'm always up for inquiries. Feel free to contact me. **AYNIW**

Contact info:
tommypopart@aol.com

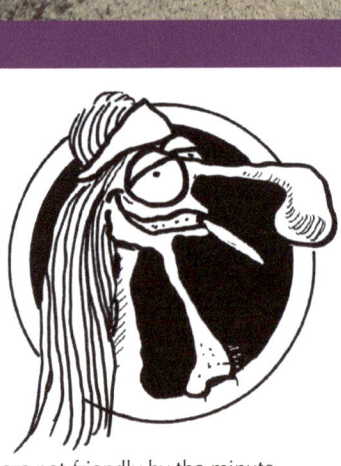

Copyright © 2017 by Tommy Pop Art, LLC

1977's *Ticket Masters:* "I literally have a box-load of comix my father had sent to me recently when he found them stored in my family's attic. They were hidden inside a stack of time-weathered newsprint pads. Some of these comix are dated, but most of the haul is still workable for the new world, which I have used to create some of what's in this book. This gem, above, is definitely a relic of the times, and you children of the 70's and 80's can relate to the good old days when you had to stand in line overnight to purchase your favorite rock band's concert tickets to get the best seats. Kinda like the way people camp out in front of the store for the new iphone, or those 'gotta-have' $500 pair of sneakers today.

Oh yeah, don't mind the typos. Remember, this piece was created by the 13-year-old in me."

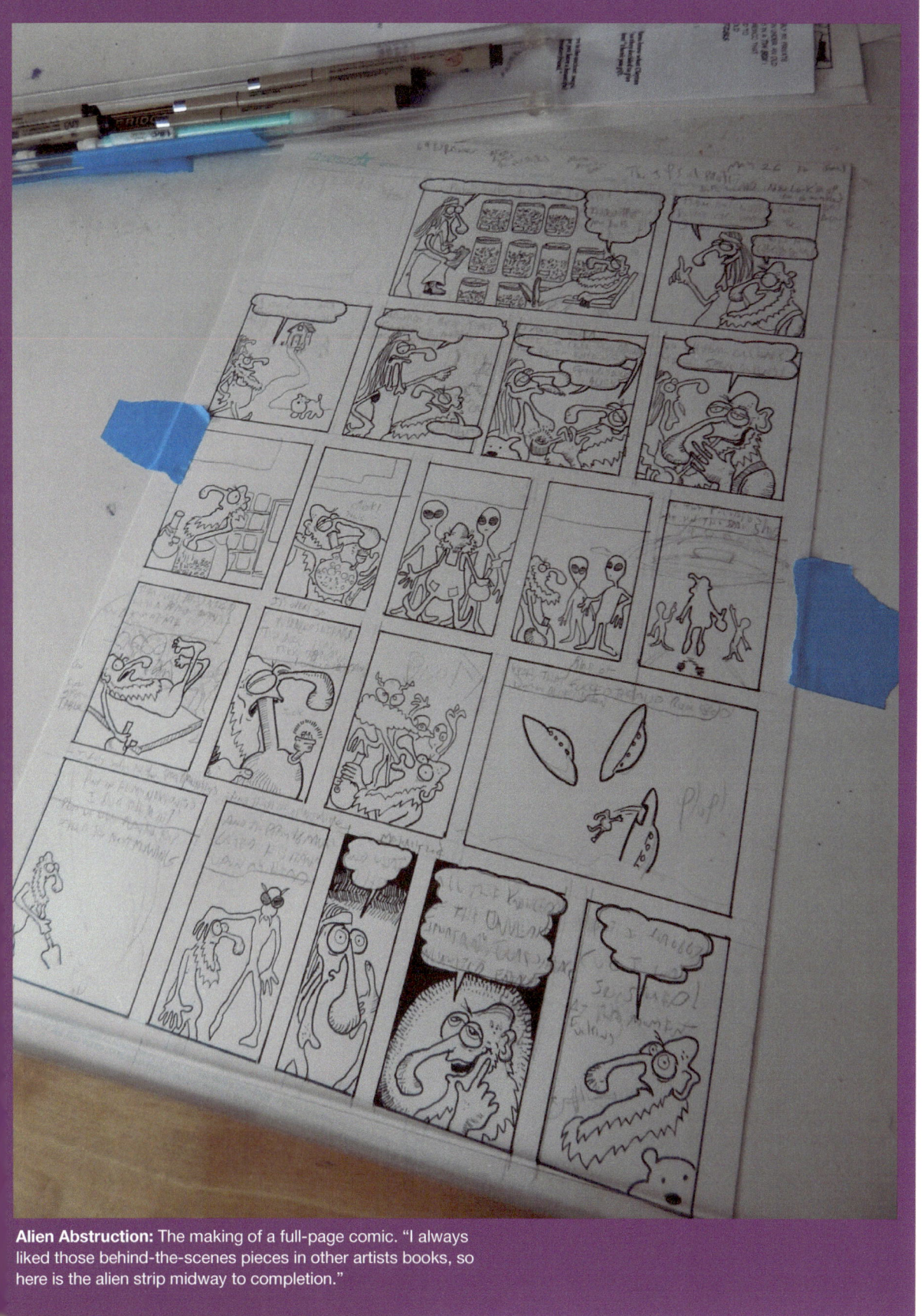

Alien Abstruction: The making of a full-page comic. "I always liked those behind-the-scenes pieces in other artists books, so here is the alien strip midway to completion."

COMIC STRIPS

ALL YOU NEED IS WEED

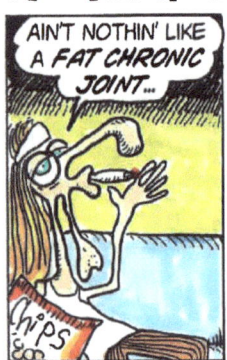
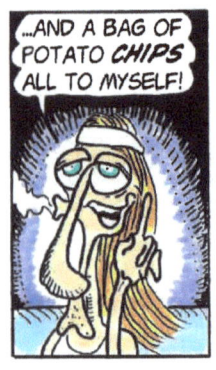
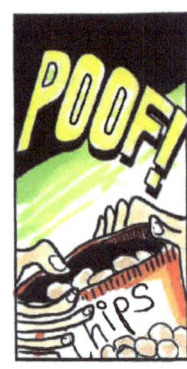
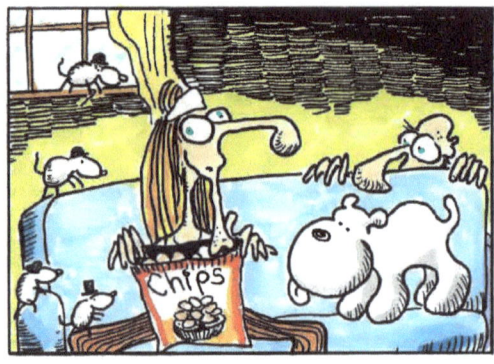

ALL YOU NEED IS WEED

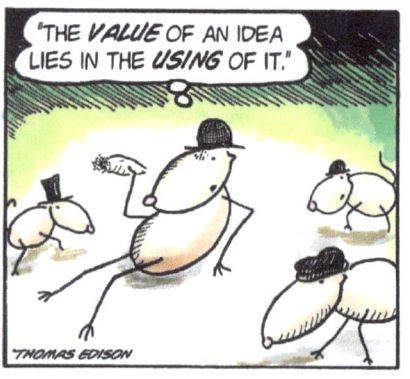
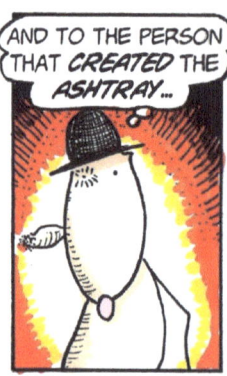
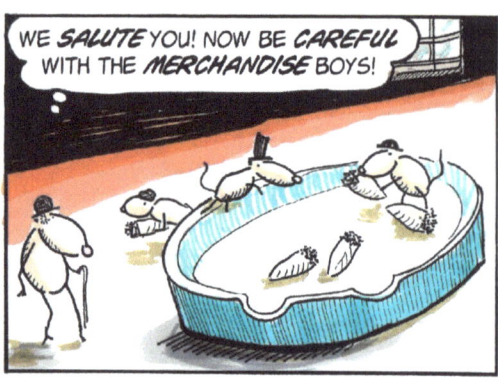

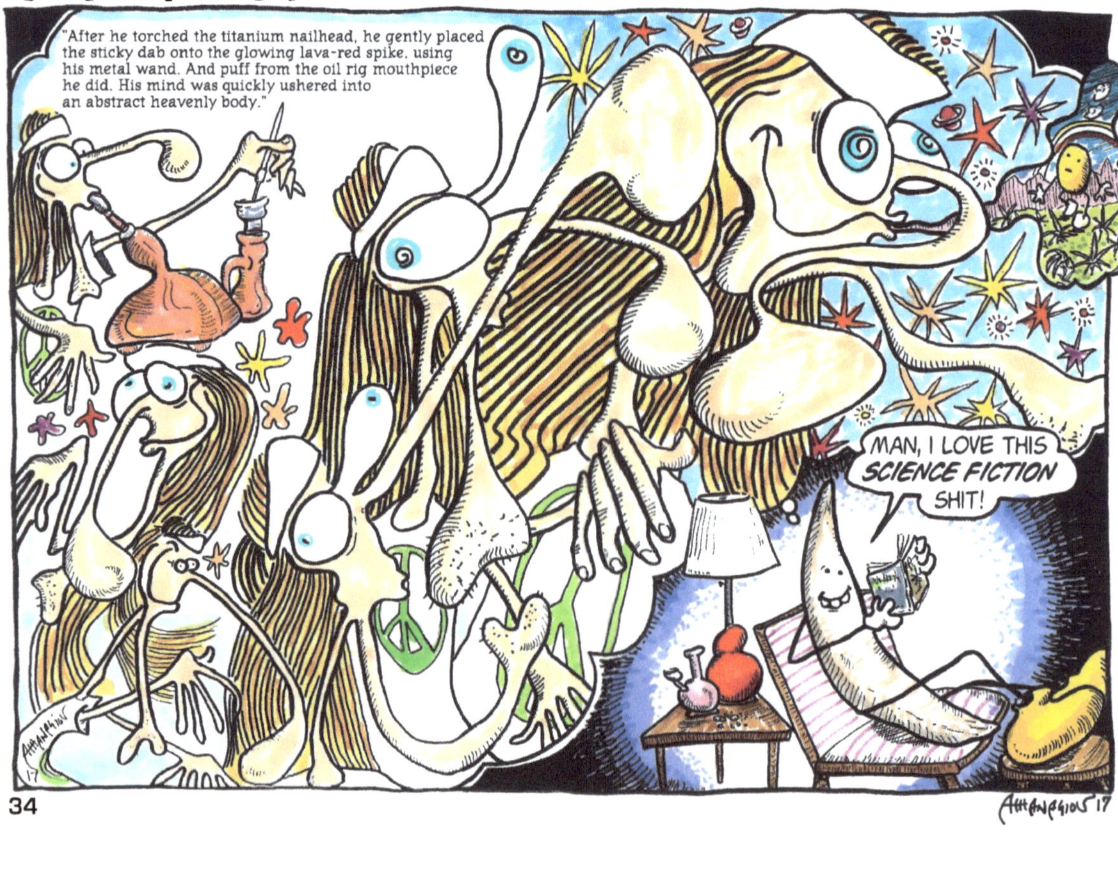

ALL YOU NEED IS WEED

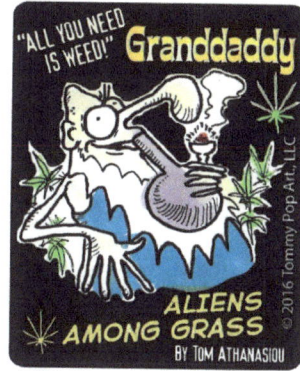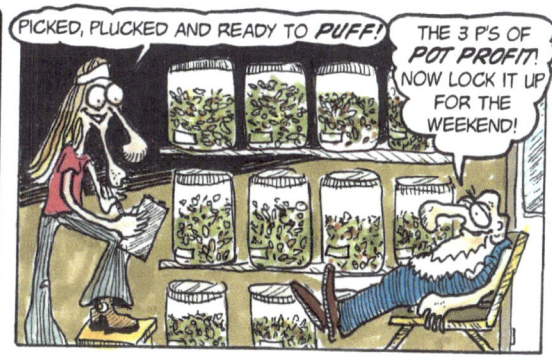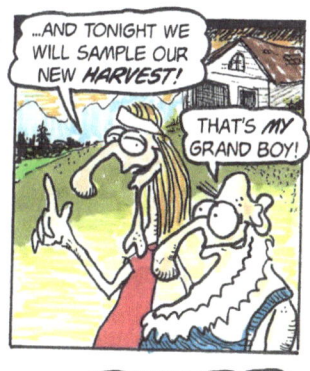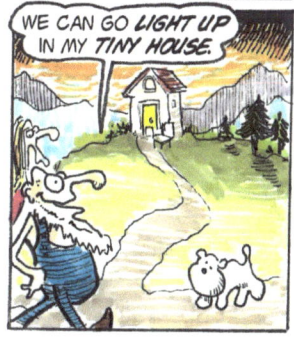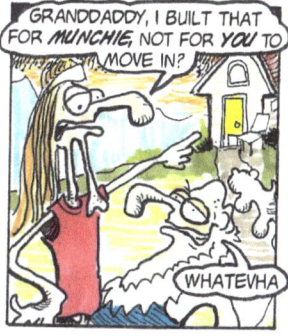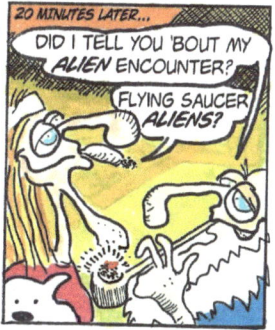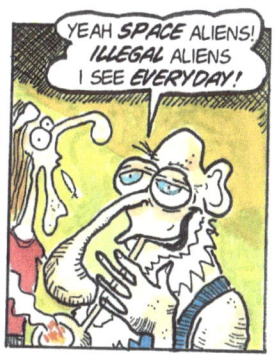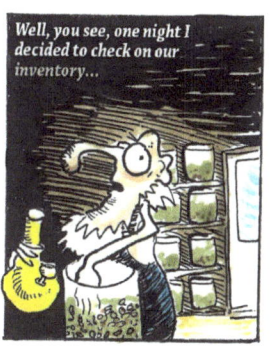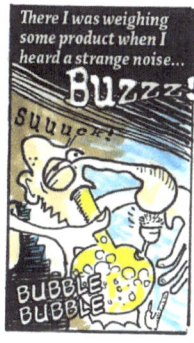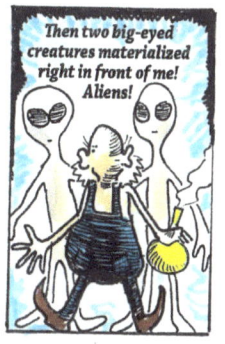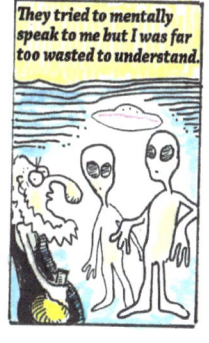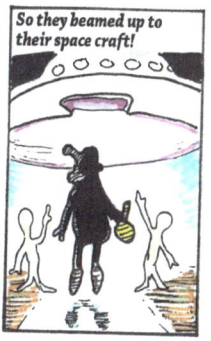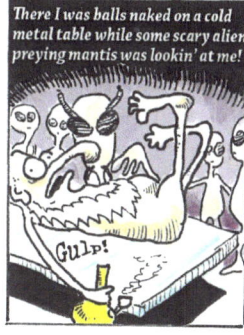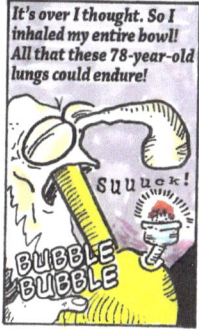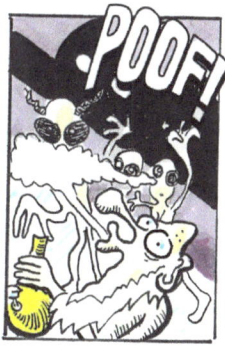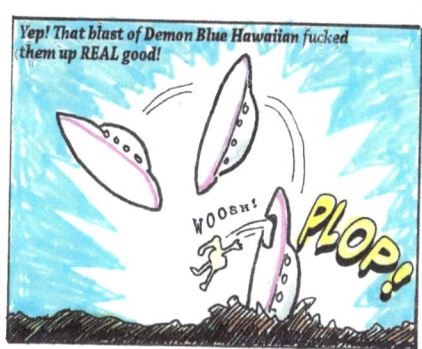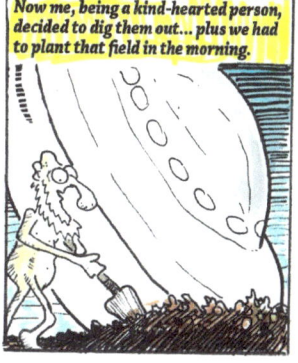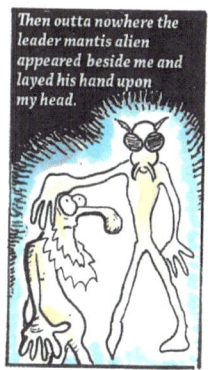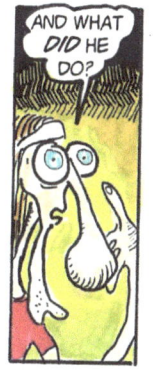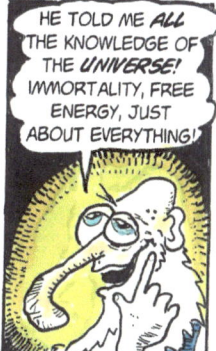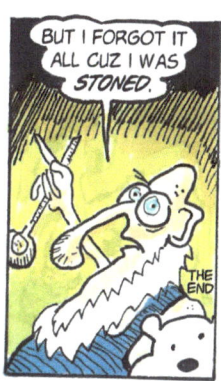

ABOUT THE ARTIST
TOM ATHANASIOU

Tom Athanasiou studied at DuCret School of Art in New Jersey where he majored in commercial art and illustration. Upon graduation, Tom headed to New York City where he found work as an assistant art director. He eventually worked for over 23 years as an executive art director in NYC and South Florida for three major magazine publishing companies, with titles including *Creem -"America's Only Rock And Roll Magazine", Iron Horse Motorcycle Magazine, Natural Woman, UFO Magazine, Hard Rock,* and a multitude of others. Additional assignments included feature illustrations, cartoons, and written articles and reviews.

Tom's recent endeavor is as the owner and artist behind the successful PITBULLSHIRT.COM, promoting "pitbull-positive" fashion designs which include shirts, hoodies, hats, and more. Ten-percent of all shirt proceeds are donated to designated pitbull rescues each month throughout the United States. He also is the author/illustrator of the popular and educational children's book series *PEANUT THE PITBULL*, which promotes pet adoption, and additionally, is the successful pop art portrait painter at TOMMYPOPART.COM.

Tom lives in South Florida with his wife, Sharon, and their two dogs.

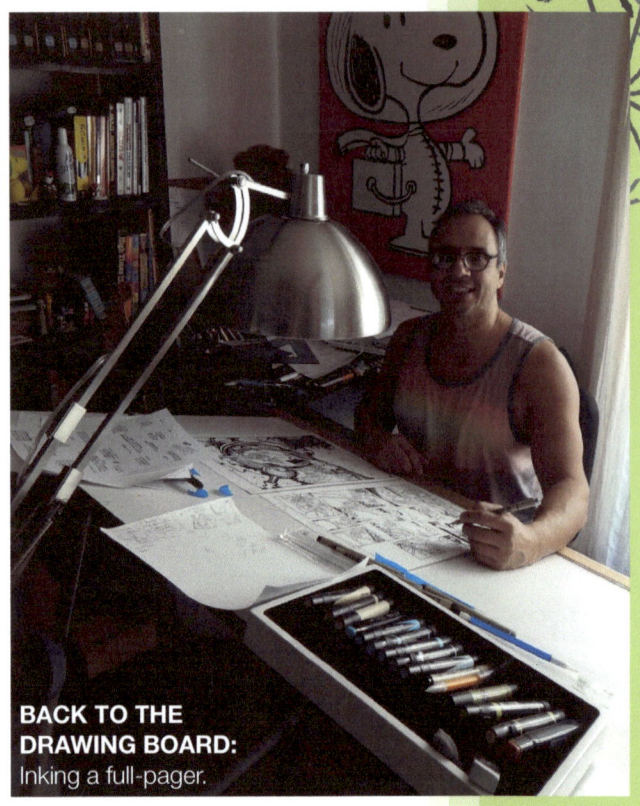

BACK TO THE DRAWING BOARD: Inking a full-pager.

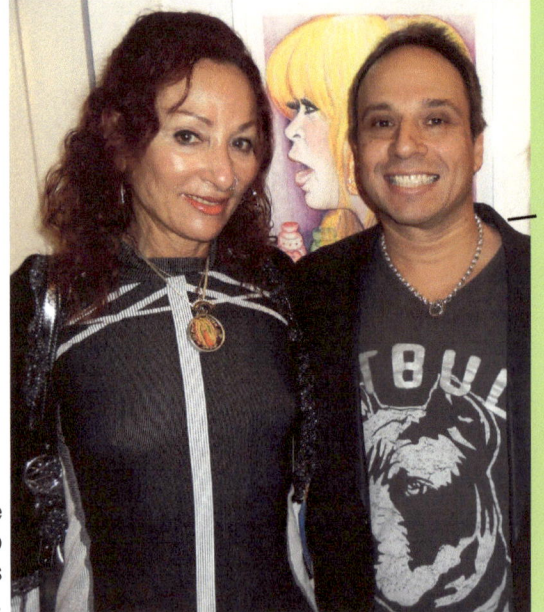

DEVIL GIRL: Aline Kominsky-Crumb and Tom at Aline's art gallery showing.

Photos by Sharon

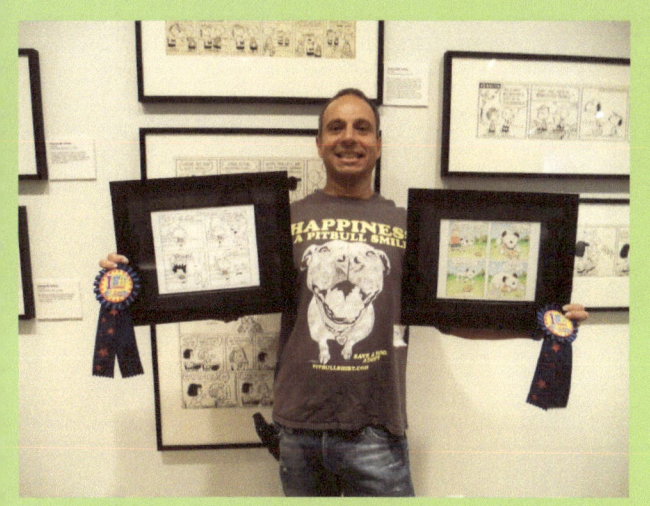
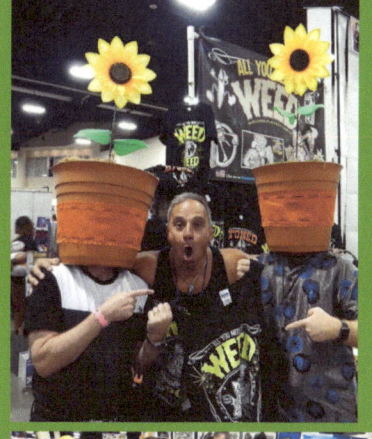
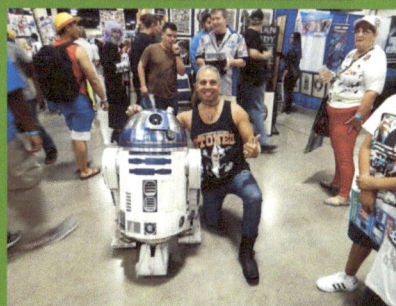

GOOD GRIEF: Tom received the award for BEST FLORIDA COMIC STRIP at the **Charles M. Schulz: Pop Culture In Peanuts** Exhibit in Hollywood, FL, for his VANILLA BEAN strip, in addition to another 1st Place BEST COMIC STRIP Award for his "Peanut The Pitbull" comic strip in the Organization/Business category which has morphed into our loveable Munchie in the *A.Y.N.I.W.* comic book series.

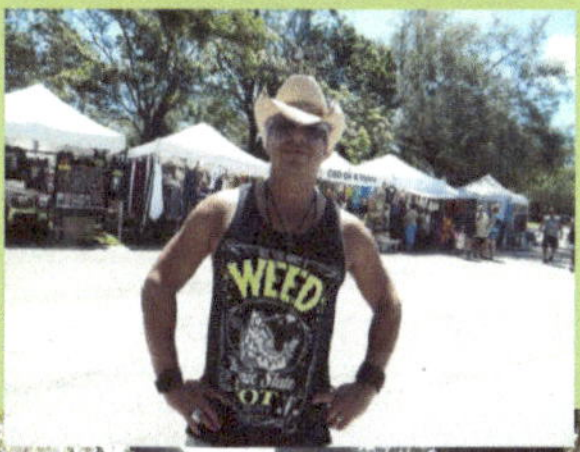

EVERYBODY MUST GET STONED: Tom and the Hippie Van at the annual LOVE-IN concert in North Miami, FL.

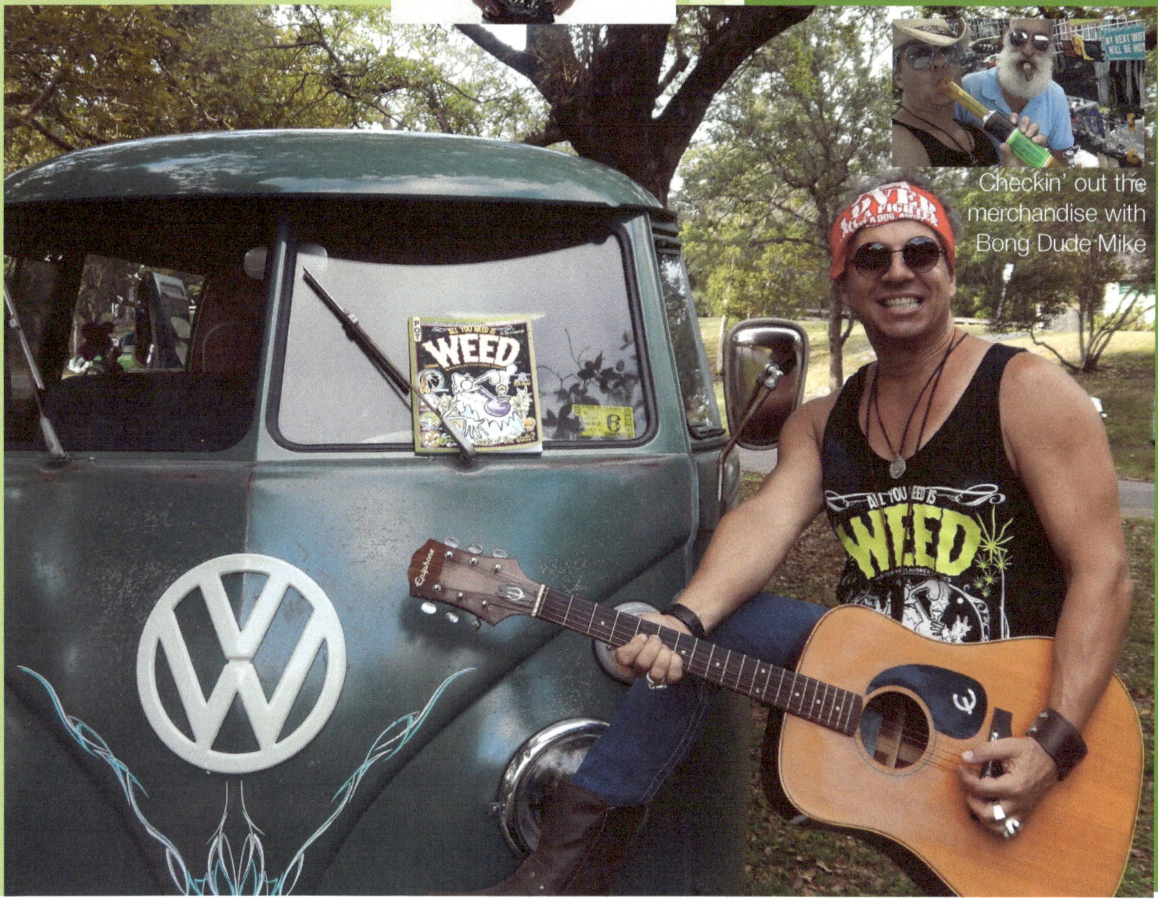

COMIC-CON: Always a blast meeting the fans at these massive events!

Checkin' out the merchandise with Bong Dude Mike

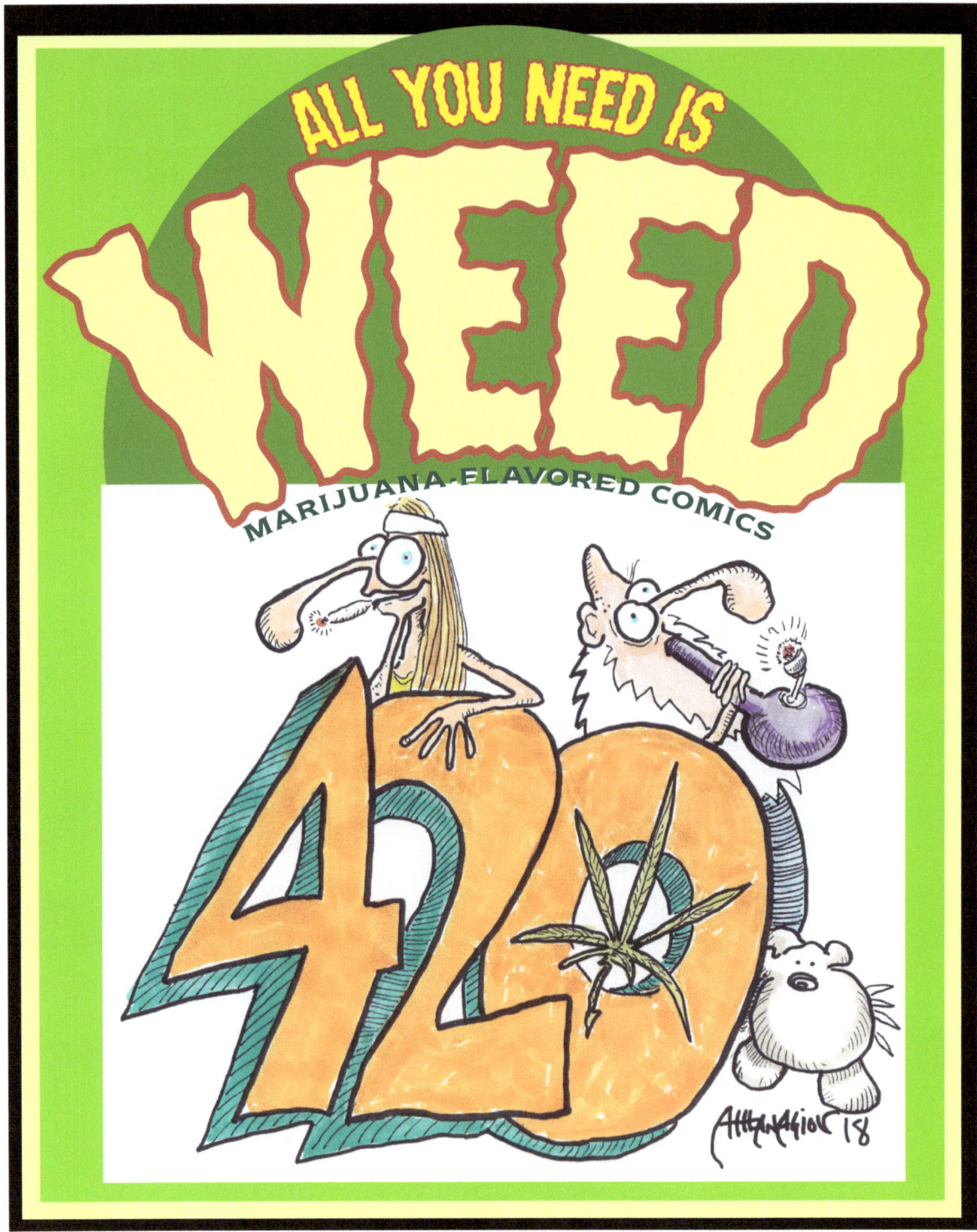

A National Holiday?: Yes! A quick little something drawn for our Facebook page on 4/20/18.

THE NEXT ISSUE

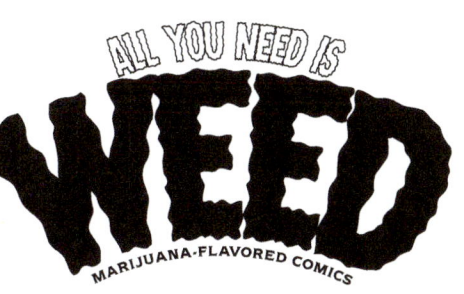

*Your underground comix weed creator Tom Athanasiou does NOT stop working folks....!

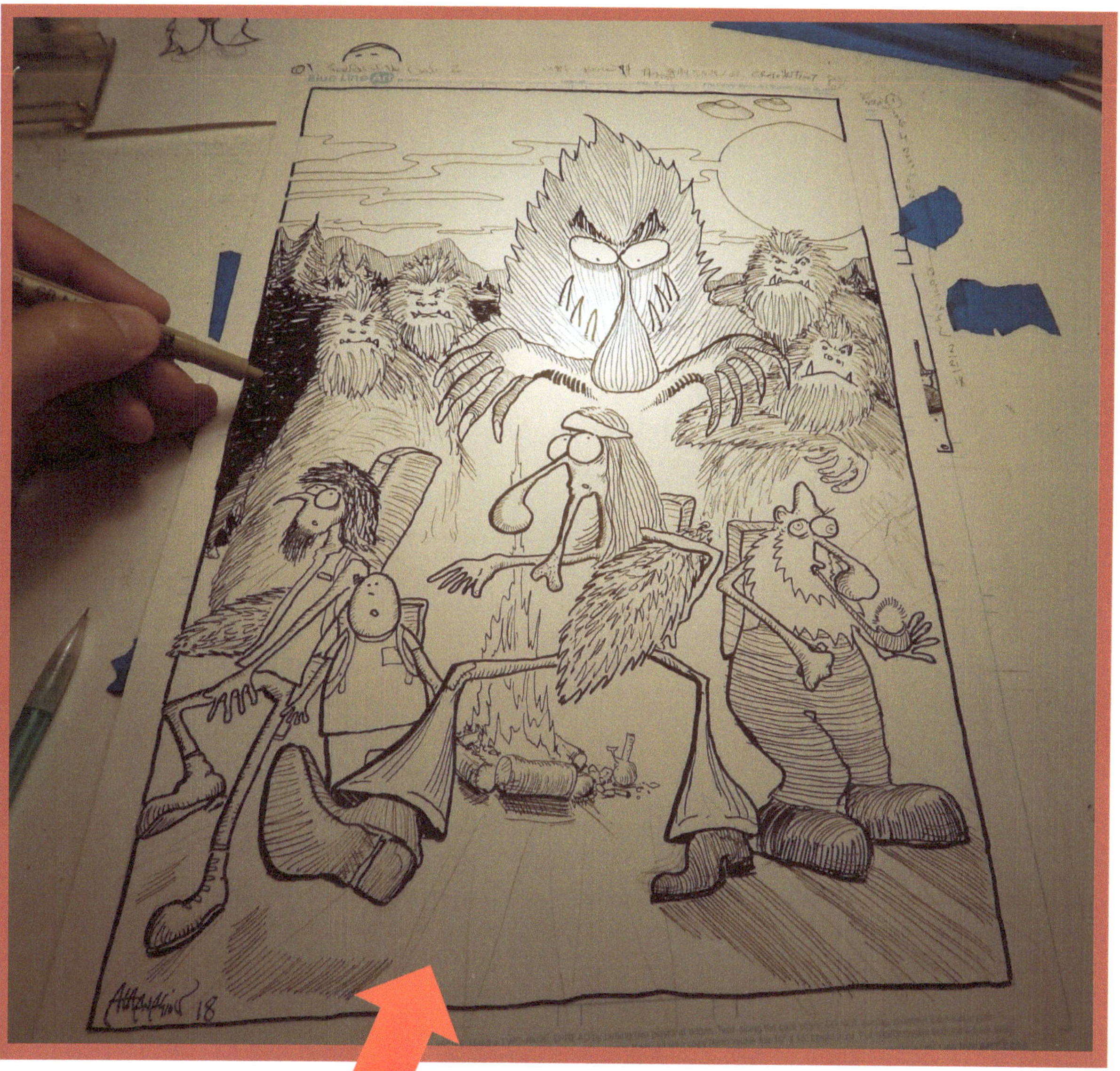

NEW STORIES!
Including...

RETURN OF THE SEEDS OF THE GODS

SHIRT SWAG

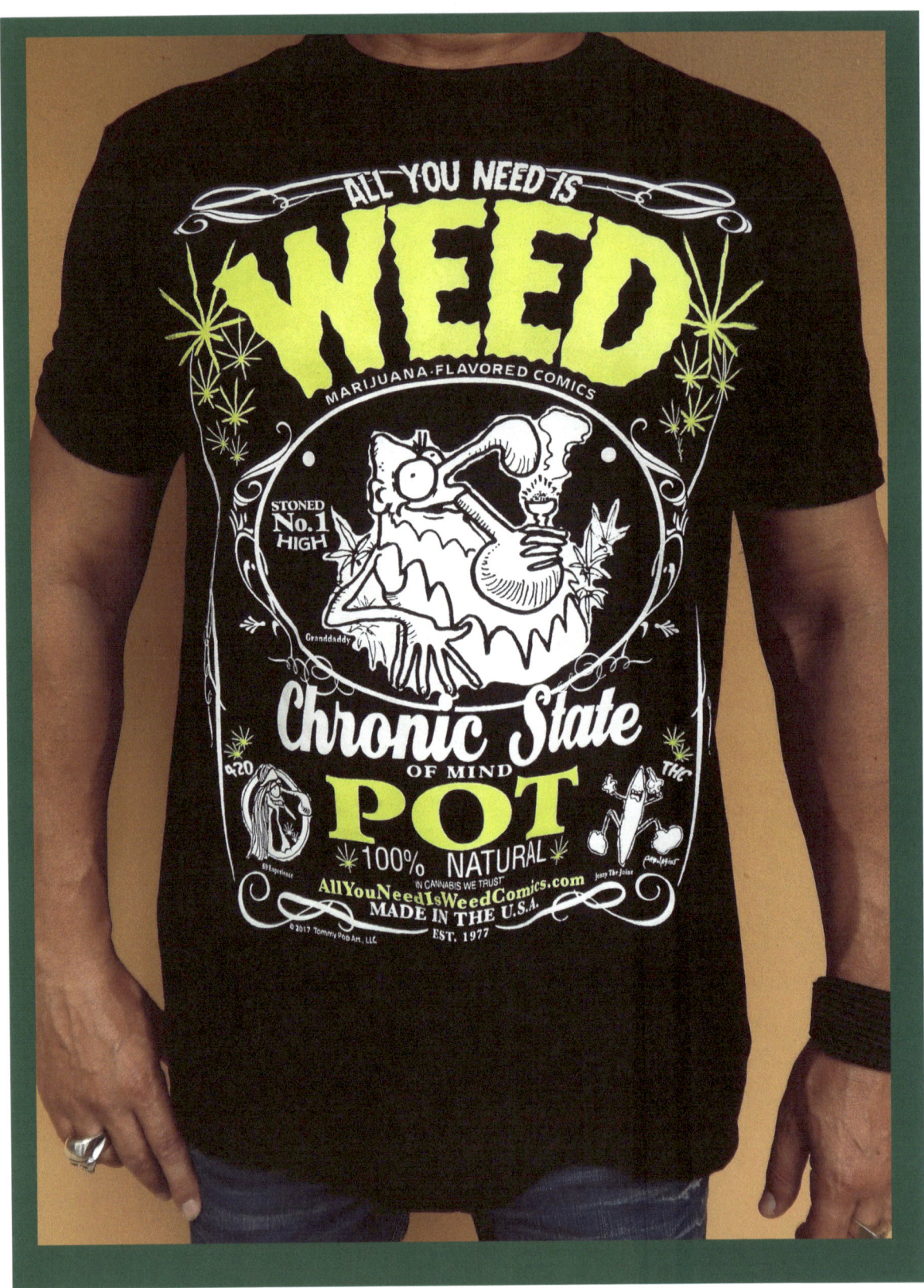

VINTAGE 70'S STYLIN'

MAKE A CHRONIC STATEMENT!

ALL YOU NEED IS WEED T-Shirts are here! Check out our website **AllYouNeedIsWeedComics.com** to find out where you can purchase them. Also, for details on new shirt designs, merchandise and Comic-cons and events we plan to attend.

SHIRTS   TANK TOPS

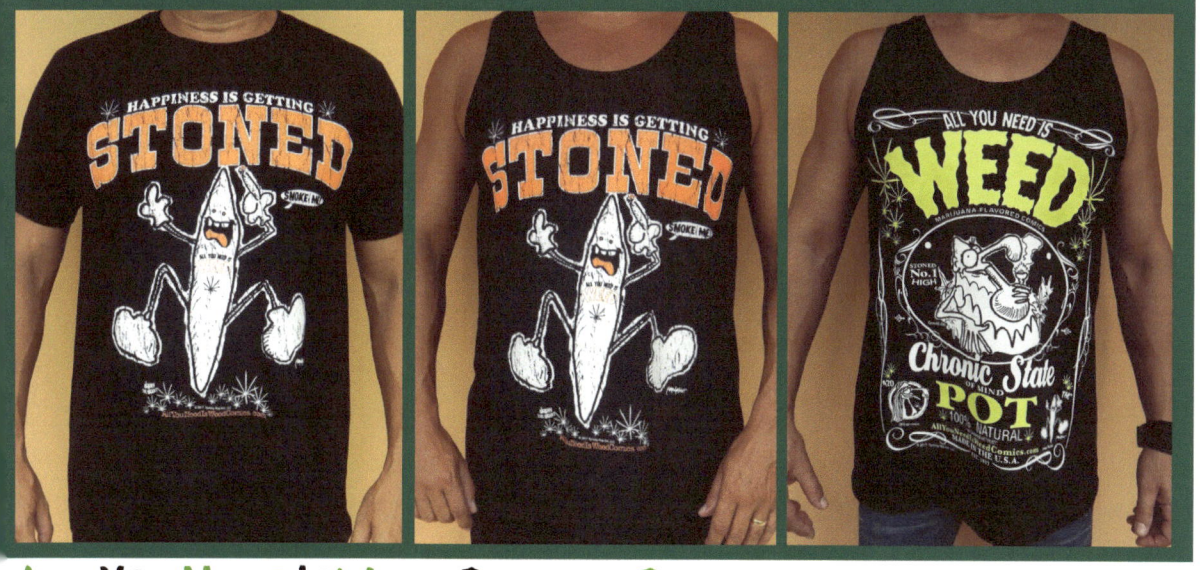

ALLYOUNEEDISWEEDCOMICS.COM

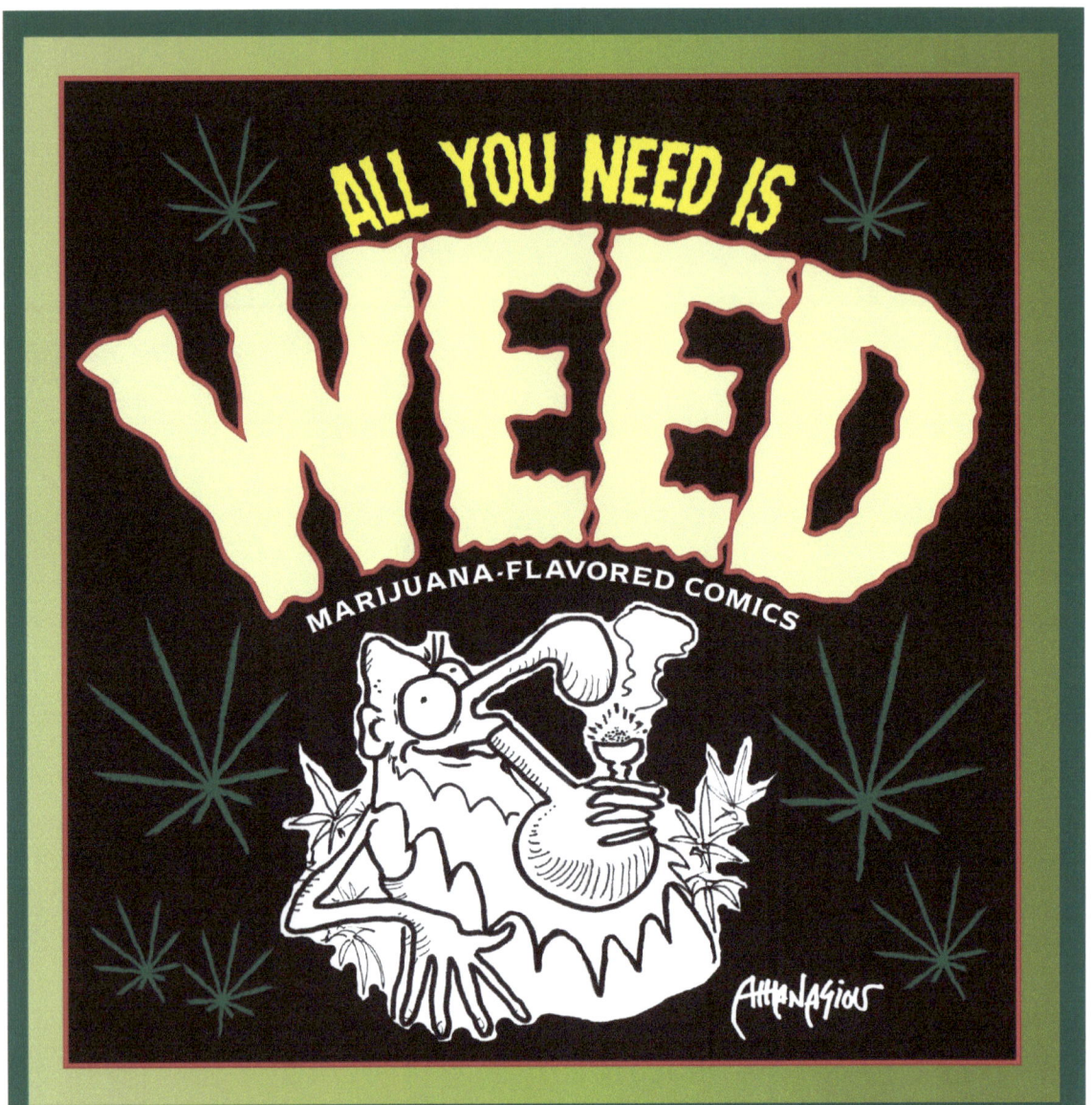

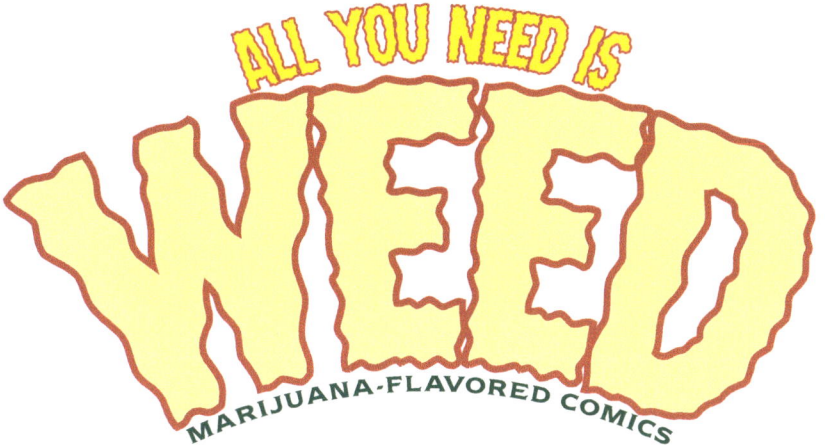

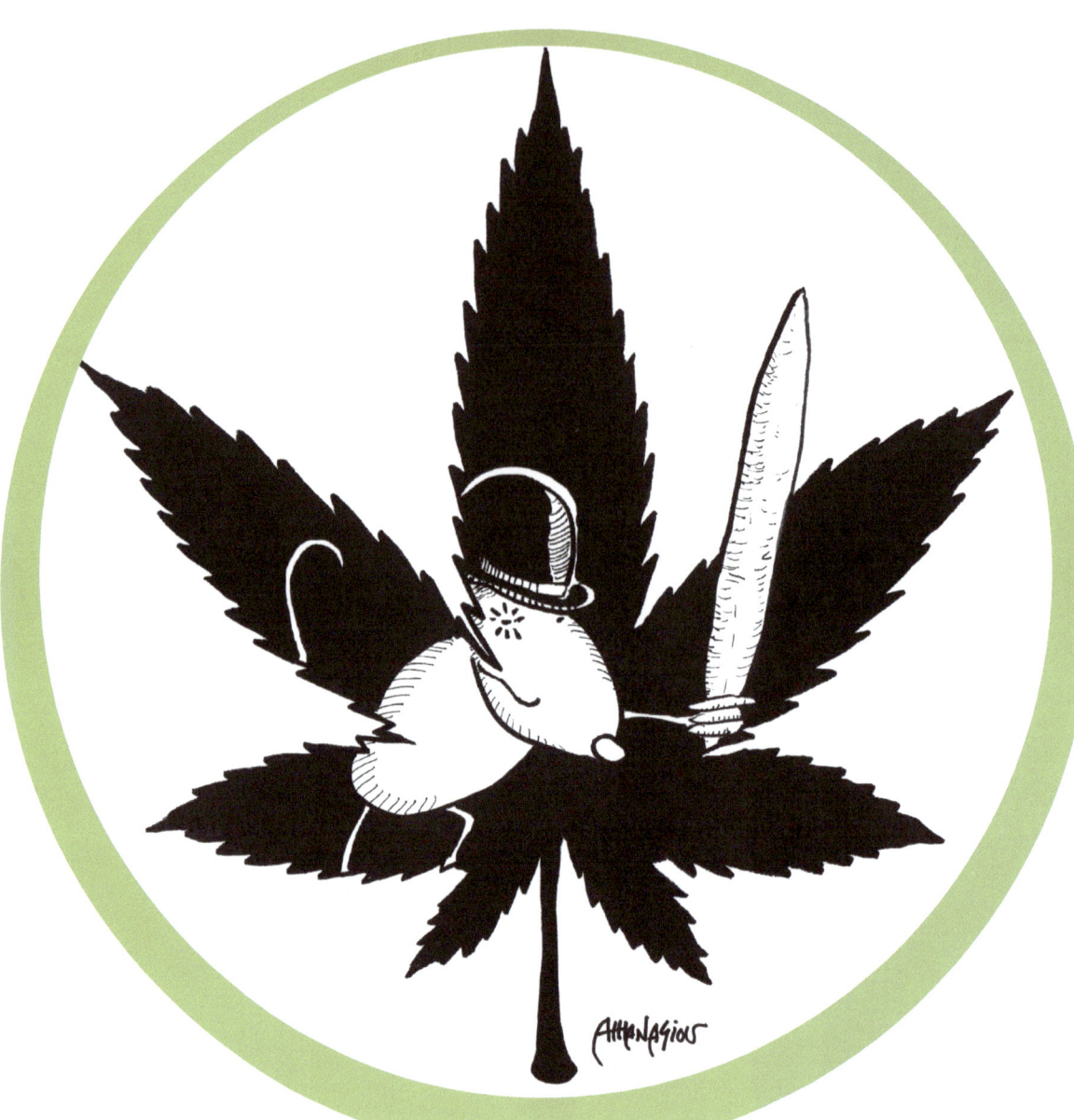

ONE LAST HIT

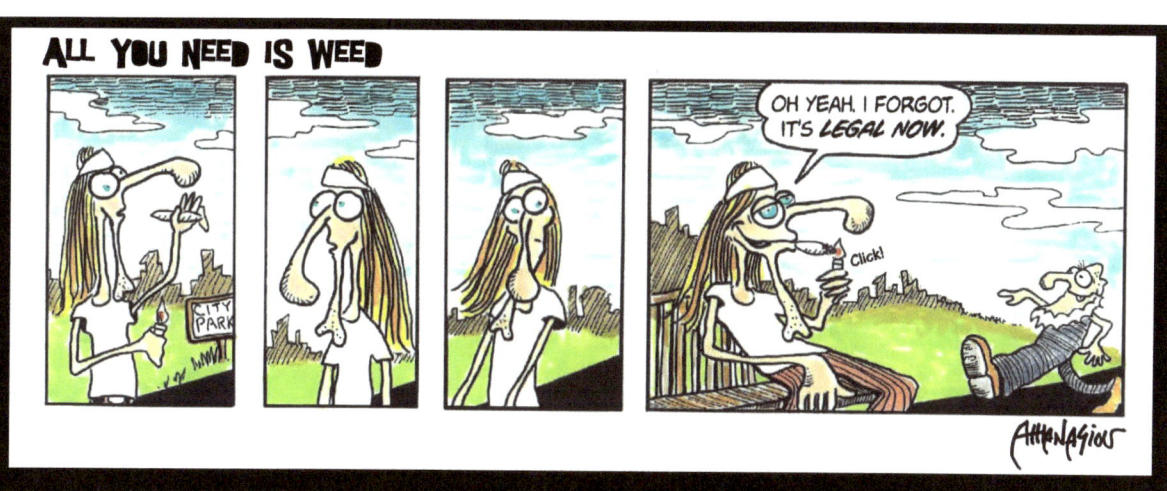

www.ingramcontent.com/pod-product-compliance
Lightning Source LLC
Chambersburg PA
CBHW042323250526
R18347300001B/R183473PG45473CBX00022B/19